BARS, TAVERNS, AND DIVES NEW YORKERS LOVE

John Tebeau

WHERE TO GO

•

BARS, TAVERNS, AND DIVES NEW YORKERS LOVE

•

WHAT TO DRINK

RIZZOLI
NEW YORK

New York · Paris · London · Milan

First published in the
United States of America in 2018
by Rizzoli International Publications, Inc.
300 Park Avenue South
New York, NY 10010
www.rizzoliusa.com

Text and illustrations © 2018 John Tebeau

2018 2019 2020 2021 / 10 9 8 7 6 5 4 3 2 1

Distributed in the U.S. trade by Random House,
New York

Printed in China
ISBN-13: 978-0-8478-6150-7

Library of Congress Catalog Control Number:
2017953318

Publisher's Note
At the time of publication, Red Lantern Bicycles
may have closed. Please confirm before visiting this
establishment or any others profiled in the book.

Book design by Sebit Min

About the Author
John Tebeau is a Brooklyn-based artist and writer. His
drawings, paintings, and prints have been shown in
New York, San Francisco, and New Orleans. He began
a series of bar illustrations in 2013 out of an appreciation of architecture and community gathering places,
later reporting on and writing about what made those
bars special. Tebeau also works as a bartender at one of
New York's great neighborhood bars, Fort Defiance in
Red Hook, Brooklyn.

TO MOM AND DAD,
who showed me how to love stuff

THE FIRST GREAT WATERING HOLE IN NEW YORK CITY was probably just that: a hole with some water in it. Maybe the water in that hole was particularly sweet, or it was situated under some shady maples, or it offered great views of the Hudson River. In any case, it was just a good place to get together and talk with your neighbors about how hot the summer had been, or the fish you caught last week, or what to do about those new people with their boats and their fancy clothes and muskets.

Since then, the city has changed. Most of the shady maples are gone, but our common human need to congregate endures, and has only gotten stronger as the city has grown. New York City offers lots of places to get together—beautiful parks, bustling avenues, museums and galleries, baseball fields and basketball courts—but I would argue that the backbone of the city's social life has always been its neighborhood restaurants and bars. Life among the city's teeming masses and glittering towers can be overwhelming; in its restaurants and bars, life resumes a human scale. In his book *The Great Good Place*, sociologist Ray Oldenburg identifies these establishments as "third places," the places between work and home, the core settings of informal public life. (Oldenburg's work inspired me to open my own neighborhood bar in Red Hook, Brooklyn, called Fort Defiance.) When they exist, they offer that increasingly rare chance to interact IRL, as the kids say; a chance to turn off the screens, to meet strangers and see familiar faces, to hear new stories and old jokes. They're the places where one leaves feeling a little more human than when one walked in, and every big city has them. Although they're often taken for granted, life without them would be unthinkable. Without them, Oldenburg says, "the urban area fails to nourish the kinds of relationships and the diversity of human contact that are the essence of the city. Deprived of these settings, people remain lonely within their crowds."

But in the overwhelming enormity of New York City, how do you find these places? One can pass dozens of bars in just a few blocks, inducing a severe case of choice paralysis. One peers in windows, looks at menu boards, and wonders: What's going on in there? Is this an old Irish pub, or a corporate facsimile? Am I dressed appropriately for this one? Can I afford this place? Most importantly: Will I be welcome here?

Good thing you've got your friend John Tebeau to show you around. And he knows what a good neighborhood joint looks like—that's one of the reasons I hired him to tend bar at mine. Now, this is not a book of New York's "best" bars, or the bars with the fanciest cocktails, or most Instagram-worthy decor. These places don't always jump and wave for your attention; they often keep a low profile. We're lucky that John has put them all here in this book, these modest beauties, and so lovingly described and drawn them, with the care an artist reserves for his favorite subjects. I know I'll use this book as intended; to get out and explore and meet some fellow New Yorkers. See you at the watering hole!

—St. John Frizell
Owner, Fort Defiance (Red Hook, Brooklyn)

MY GRANDPA OWNED a couple of speakeasies in Detroit during the twenties. In the fifties my dad opened a restaurant and later a saloon in my hometown, Muskegon, Michigan. "Going out" was a regular thing we did when I was a kid, and Mom and Dad often took us to wonderful places like Fricano's Pizzeria, Aaron's White Kitchen, and the Bear Lake Tavern. I loved those visits. We had a blast seeing people, being seen, playing tabletop shuffle bowling and video games, feeding the jukebox, and eating like kings. That early influence is probably why I still love going out (and *hanging* out), especially where I feel at home.

We need that here in New York, that *being at home* feeling, in this huge, heaving city, where most of us are from someplace else. We're all working and sweating and commuting and hustling, constantly trying to find and keep our footing. We need places where we can feel grounded. Many of us live in small apartments, so for our mental and spiritual well-being we've gotta have a little more room. Extra space to occasionally call our own, chill out, and just be. "Third places," as Ray Oldenburg called them in his excellent book *The Great Good Place: Cafes, Coffee Shops, Bookstores, Bars, Hair Salons, and Other Hangouts at the Heart of a Community*; not home, not work, but someplace else, where somebody (if not everybody) knows your name.

The good news is there are thousands of these all over New York City. Bars, cafés, clubs, coffee shops, churches/temples/mosques, diners, bowling alleys, and scores more to suit every interest and inclination. I like bars and taverns (maybe passed on by my dad and grandpa), not so much for the drinking, but for comfort, company, and atmosphere. I love that warm, homey feeling you get when you have bonded with other folks who work or hang out at a particular place—when they know and care about you.

Bars, Taverns, and Dives New Yorkers Love profiles some of the favorite (*favorite*, not *best*, which is waaaayy too subjective to even seriously contemplate) drinking establishments of NYC. It's an outgrowth of an art project I started a couple of years ago, drawing and making prints of my six favorite joints in Brooklyn, my home borough. People bought those prints (and others, as the project expanded) out of real affection for these places. Maybe it was where they went on a first date, fell in love, or held their wedding reception. Sometimes it was a gift for their dad/best friend/partner, a souvenir of a favorite hangout or the good old days. But it was always out of affection. Like it says in the title, these are places New Yorkers *love*.

John Tebeau
Brooklyn, New York

ADOBE BLUES

63 Lafayette Avenue (at Fillmore Street) NEW BRIGHTON, STATEN ISLAND
adobeblues.com · *718-720-2583*

"IT'S JUST A GREAT NEIGHBORHOOD PLACE. A place people like to go. It's like . . . it's like fuckin' *Cheers*." That's how regular Doug Kenny described Adobe Blues one Sunday evening as I sat at the bar, enjoying my Mexican Firing Squad, a well-made cocktail classic featuring tequila, fresh-squeezed lime juice, and grenadine. The regulars love this place so much that an online #SaveAdobe campaign helped scuttle a 2015 deal to sell it, according to general manager Jack Dabdoub.

Adobe has an old-timey southwestern saloon bar up front and a dining room in back. The place smells wholesomely of Tex-Mex food, with spicy overtones of good beer and tequila. The saloon can get loud, but not with music. Fun-loud with conversation—more like a series of big-voice DECLA-RATIONS!—by the regulars. As a visiting Brooklynite (complete with dweeby glasses), I felt a little overwhelmed at first, like the history prof at a hockey game, but hey—everyone was having a fine time, myself included. It felt like being at the tail end of a rowdy family holiday party.

Adobe is a thoroughly beloved neighborhood bar. I don't see many places of its caliber in that regard, and I've been looking. It's a locals place, with lots of ribbing and shouting and jokes and backslapping, but it's welcoming to visitors, too. Do yourself a favor and seek these places out. Maybe you won't be-come a regular because they're too far away. Maybe you'll only hit them once, or once a year, but spots like Adobe Blues are good for the soul and showcase the best of what a great neighborhood bar is all about—a place for human connection and society, and, in a way, an extension of home.

Adobe Blues is also a hell of a craft beer bar, one of New York's best since it opened in 1994, well before most of the other NYC beer geeks got around to opening their own places. There's a huge selection of bottles and cans, plus five taps, and the bar hosts an annual brewery appreciation day, when craft breweries from all over set up shop, offer samples, and answer your questions. What Adobe Blues *isn't* is pretentious or stuffy, like some beer-snob bars can be, or "douchey," in the words of bartender Hannah Spisto. Hear, hear!

THE DECOR *is the* MAIN THING FIRST-TIME VISITORS NOTICE, ACCORDING *to* BAR MANAGER RYAN BARKER. THE PLACE IS SO LOADED *with* CURIOSITIES, KEEPSAKES, *and* BRIC-A-BRAC THAT EVEN STAFFERS WHO'VE WORKED HERE FOR YEARS SOMETIMES NOTICE ITEMS THEY'VE MISSED.

ADOBE BLUES

WHEN TO GO	Bar manager Ryan Barker suggests you stop by during the late afternoon or on a Monday or Tuesday evening, when it's not too busy. Spend some time learning about Adobe's massive beer selection. With the bartender's help, try some brews you've never had or even heard of before. Bartender Hannah Spisto recommends Sunday afternoons, when Adobe Blues is jumping with both brunchers and drinkers. Wednesday nights are a fan favorite, too, when longtime house band the Wolfpack plays jazz and blues from nine to midnight.
WHERE TO SIT	"George's seat," Barker tells me, "where you can see everything." It's at the end of the bar close to the door. Go ahead and sit there, but if George shows up, you might have to move. Don't say you weren't warned.
WHAT TO DRINK	Get a beer. They have almost two hundred to choose from, so dig deep. At quieter times, when beer aficionado Barker is working, he'll guide you to surprising brews, like the Rothaus Pils Tannenzäpfle ("The Original Beer from Germany's Black Forest") that I tried, or something equally exotic from the wilds of, say, Brooklyn. And also, because man cannot live on beer alone, order the house margarita: they make a good one, and hey, you're in a *cantina*, after all.

HOUSE RECIPE

Adobe Blues Margarita

2 ounces tequila
1 ounce Cointreau or triple sec
1 ounce sour mix
½ ounce fresh lime juice

Shake all the ingredients with ice in a cocktail shaker. Strain and serve over ice in a rocks glass with a salted rim.

HOW TO GET THERE	It's an easy place to love, Adobe Blues, if not all that easy to get to— unless, of course, you happen to be a neighborhood regular. But getting there is half the fun! Take the (free) Staten Island Ferry from Lower Manhattan, enjoying the ride and the views of Manhattan, Brooklyn, and the Statue of Liberty, then order a car for the remaining mile-and-a-half ride to Adobe (or get the S44 bus from the ferry, which drops you off across the street). Or, if you have a bike and the weather's decent, bring it on the ferry and pedal.

THE ATLANTIC CHIPSHOP

129 Atlantic Avenue (between Clinton and Henry Streets) BROOKLYN HEIGHTS, BROOKLYN
chipshopnyc.com · *718-855-7775*

"YOU DON'T MESS WITH Susan unless you want a bruisin'." So says bartender Liz Drobits with respect to her co-worker Suzy Hackett. Lady bartenders rule the roost at the Atlantic ChipShop in Brooklyn Heights, and owner Chris Sell likes it that way. "Strong women bartenders keep the crowd in line," he says.

It's rare that the crowd at ChipShop gets *too* out of line, though, and I should know. It's my local lunch spot of choice, just down the street from our apartment. It's generally not overly packed, never too quiet, and always a fine place to while away a lunch hour or two. At times, with the right mix of customers, you get classic, wise-ass, local-bar banter. The kind where smart people make dumb jokes, and they know each other well enough to push the line a bit, with a little wholesome cursing and somewhat off-color comments, but never *too* off-color, especially when Hackett's working, because, you know, you don't want to risk a *bruisin'*.

Sell, who hails from Warwickshire, England, opened the place in 2005 with Brooklyn barman Bobby Gagnon, and his vision for the ChipShop was simple: a British pub with British food and lots of British beverages. "I wanted to have a bar where fathers could bring their sons to watch the game," he says. "It took over a year to open because we were idiots." It worked out, eventually, and the place is currently hitting on all one cylinder, not unlike the mighty ChipShopmobile, a fiberglass hunk of three-wheeled raw power that you'll often see parked out front on Atlantic Avenue.

The feel of the place is right. It smells good and fried inside. The music is bartender-driven, a generally palatable mix of eighties Brit pop, classic seventies stuff, and of course some Beatles. There's a modest bar up front, a dining room in back, and posters of Brits all over the walls—the Who, Black Sabbath, Siouxsie Sioux, the Sex Pistols chewing their nails and grabbing their groins. Sean Connery as James Bond, John Paul George & Ringo, David Bowie in a bomber jacket, heroically hoisting a pint. Benny Hill, Dr. Who, the Monty Python gang. Some kings and queens are up there, too, on collectible plates.

And what's surprising, given the thorough bad-mouthing that British food receives, is how bloody solid the kitchen actually is. The fish and chips are reliably excellent, the cod hot and moist inside a crispy cocoon of golden-fried batter and buttressed with a hefty serving of thick-cut fries with a little cup of curry-laced tartar sauce on the side. The shepherd's pie, including the veggie version, is volcanic, rich, creamy, and satisfying. In fact, my wife, Colleen, who's a vegetarian, eats like a queen at ChipShop; their mushroom mac and cheese is one of her go-to comfort foods. Point is, you'll not only drink well at ChipShop, you'll eat well, too. Scotch eggs, Welsh rarebit, bangers and mash, bubble and squeak: ChipShop's got you covered. But forget about hamburgers, mate. "I've never put a burger on the menu, and I never will," says Sell. That's Yank food. Go get that at Shake Shack.

FOR A MODEST FEE, THE KITCHEN WILL DEEP-FRY ANYTHING YOU BRING THEM. DEEP-FRIED CANDY BARS LIKE SNICKERS, TWIX, and REESE'S PEANUT BUTTER CUPS ARE ALWAYS on the MENU. BUT SERIOUSLY, IF YOU BRING IN A NATHAN'S HOT DOG, THEY'LL BATTER AND FRY IT. A BANANA, NO PROBLEM. A BIG, GOOEY POPCORN BALL LEFT OVER from HALLOWEEN? CONSIDER IT DONE.

WHEN TO GO	Hit the ChipShop for lunch on a Friday when you have a little time to kill. Sit at the bar and avail yourself of their daily, all-afternoon happy hour. Engage in some conversation with the regulars, chat with the bartender, or just read. Bonus: If there's a British soccer—excuse me, *football*—match that day, the place fills up with fans and the shop goes from a quiet little pub to a just-rowdy-enough footie bar. *Happy hour: Monday to Friday, noon to 7 p.m., 20 percent off everything (drinks and food) when you sit at the bar.*
WHERE TO SIT	Anytime, day or night, the best seat in the house is the end of the bar, to your right as you walk in the door—except when you're in the mood for a little privacy. In that case, go for the booth in the front window, under the Sex Pistols poster. Nothing says intimacy like Johnny Rotten biting his nails above you.
WHAT TO DRINK	Start with either beer or cider. Follow that up with either cider or beer. Sell is adamant that this place is an *English* pub, dammit, and he stocks the beer and cider to prove it. There are seventeen on tap and one cask. Looking for an IPA—or a big, bitter, smack-you-in-the-gob Oregon hop bomb? Good luck. Sell begrudgingly keeps a couple American IPAs on tap for the Yanks, but you might want to dig into the British selections. A Kilkenny cream ale or O'Hara stout will do the trick, and when it comes to cider, you'll usually find Aspall and Strongbow on tap, with ten or so more options available in bottles.

Subway: The 2, 3, 4, and 5 trains all stop at the Borough Hall station, and the R train stops at Court Street–Borough Hall, all about a ten-minute walk to ChipShop.

Take a look at ChipShop's tabletops. Many are kaleidoscopic works of collage art, made by Sell and encased in clear acrylic. British pound notes, British postage stamps, scores of British coins from the old, pre-decimalization days of the British monetary system—Sell arranged them with precision, and they're really quite striking to behold. Look carefully, and if—among all those pounds and pence and farthings and whatnot—you can find the *one* U.S. coin in the whole lot (a 1943 wartime steel penny), then you win . . . nothing.

Overheard at ChipShop:

On Rugby vs. Football
Suzy Hackett, bartender: "We get more random people in here for football games than rugby. More people understand the rules of football. I prefer the rugby crowd. More regulars."
N. C., regular: "She likes the bigger asses on rugby players. But don't quote me."
Hackett: "That is also true."

On the Splendor of ChipShop
Nate Chavkin (no relation to N. C., honest), regular: "This is one of the few bars I come to in Brooklyn where I don't want to cry."
Neal Boulton, regular: "It's a great forum for ideas. It's more like a social club than a bar. You know, like in ancient Greece, where they got together to share ideas? With wise men? Only here, not so wise. . . ."
Someone else: "Wise guys."

On the Subtle Distinctions of Various British Beers
Customer: "What's the difference between the Fuller's London Pride and the Fuller's ESB?"
"Brooklyn Frankie," bartender emeritus: "They're two different fuckin' beers."

On Politics
"We assert ourselves politically here," says Sell, referencing the IMMIGRANT AND PROUD *buttons they sell at the bar for a buck apiece. As an immigrant himself from the English town of Rugby, he takes the issue seriously. "Maybe we shouldn't, but we do." On Inauguration Day 2017, Chip-Shop ran a nonstop* Monty Python *marathon, balm for the souls of many regulars.*

BAR GREAT HARRY

280 Smith Street (at Sackett Street) · CARROLL GARDENS, BROOKLYN
bargreatharry.com · *347-457-5650*

IT WAS FATED THAT BAR GREAT HARRY would open on the corner of Sackett and Smith, in Brooklyn's Carroll Gardens neighborhood, a traditional Italian enclave that has changed a lot over the past couple decades. Back in 2006 Ben and Mike Wiley saw that transformation up close. The brothers lived in the neighborhood, and Ben bartended at Abilene, a neighborhood bar on Court Street. In those days they hung out a lot on Smith Street, Carroll Gardens' bar/restaurant strip, and realized the need for a good, no-frills craft beer bar. "No TVs, no Stella" was the vision. They just needed a location. And money. And a business plan. But all that would come. At least they had a vision. Then, almost mystically, they found the perfect location.

Ben explains: "We're drinking one night at what we called 'Bar Bar,' this place at two-eighty Smith with no real name. It's two a.m. on a weeknight, and we see an older man in a sport coat at the end of the bar, talking to the bartender. I say to Mike, 'See that guy? I bet he's the owner.' So he goes outside for a smoke, and my brother and I go out, too. I kinda sidle up to him and say, 'I wanna buy your bar.' He takes a drag, pauses, and says, 'Really? I want to *sell* my bar.' Within three months we got the keys." Easy.

And it's easy to feel at home when you walk into Bar Great Harry, too. The front "wall" mostly consists of French doors, and in decent weather they're wide open. Accessibility is what it's all about here at this public house. People love it "because they feel comfortable in here," says Ben. "We try to make it a comfortable place to catch up with people from your neighborhood, from the music to the lighting to the bartenders, the decor—everything."

And it works. I found that out a few years back, when my wife and I popped in after work one day, took two seats at the high wooden bar, and slid into a perfect happy hour. "I'm Blue" by the Shangri-Las moaned through speakers above the bar, the first of many tunes I adopted from BGH for my own playlists. Folks played some intense pinball in the back room. Up front, all the doors were open, and a couple dogs hung out with their people. I enjoyed an exotic stout of some kind, while my beer-loathing wife sipped a whiskey sour, taking advantage of the happy hour discount on well drinks at this corner bar in the heart of the neighborhood.

WITH THREE MACHINES in the BACK ROOM, BAR GREAT HARRY IS
A HUB IN THE WORLD OF NEW YORK PINBALL, HOSTING LEAGUE MATCHES
ALL SEASON LONG. I'VE BEEN THERE for LEAGUE PLAY,
WHERE THE MATCHES ARE LOOSE, SPIRITED, AND ROWDY.

Ben Wiley suggests two to five in the afternoon, "when it's slow, and everyone is there because they love the place."

Happy hour: Monday to Friday, 2 to 7 p.m. $1 off all drinks, beer, wine, and shots.

Sit at one of the rough-hewn little tables by the French doors facing Smith Street, an especially fine spot when the weather is mild, the doors are open, and the street life of Carroll Gardens rolls on by you all evening.

First try the beer-and-a-shot special, and not your average swill, either. "It's good!" Ben says. "It'll be oddball, high-quality stuff, which always changes." Then go deeper into the beer list, or try a glass of wine on draft. Bar Great Harry stocks no bottles, but always features five or six New York State varieties on tap. *Wine on tap?* Yes. There's almost no oxidation, so you'll get a remarkably fresh-tasting pour.

Subway: The F and G trains stop just a few blocks south at the Carroll Street station.

It's a weird name, Bar Great Harry. The Wileys borrowed it from a cocktail bar in Yokohama, Japan, where Ben got a graduate degree in Japanese Studies while bartending at night. "Their story was that there was some old famous British navy ship called *Great Harry* that used to dock in Yokohama," he explains. "This regular old Japanese dude that owned the bar decided to name it Bar Great Harry, I guess because he liked that ship. When Mike and I were brainstorming names, he said to me one day, 'Fuck it, let's call it Bar Great Harry.' We kind of looked at each other and giggled, and that was that."

Bar Great Harry used to be known as one of the premier dog-friendly bars of Brooklyn. While allowing dogs inside bars was always against the New York City Department of Health's rules, it wasn't strictly enforced, so Bar Great Harry (and a lot of other bars of New York) let people hang indoors with their well-mannered dogs. That changed with New York City's bar and restaurant grading system and increasingly frequent crackdowns by the Department of Health for dog-in-bar violations. If multiple busts happened, "we couldn't renew our insurance," says Ben. "And in the bar business, insurance is everything."

BARBÈS

376 Ninth Street (at Sixth Avenue)   SOUTH SLOPE, BROOKLYN
barbesbrooklyn.com   ·   *347-422-0248*

BARBÈS (YOU SAY IT "BAR-*BESS*") IS A SURPRISE. A throwback. A scruffy little music club, the kind you might've found in the East Village in the nineties, with funk and soul, and it's hidden in plain sight at the cusp of South Slope and Park Slope proper in Brooklyn. Right there, among the many multimillion-dollar brownstones and all those strollers and babies and nannies and yellow Labs, there's a seriously cool music scene happening.

Every night in Barbès's tight little back room, musicians play. No cover, no tickets—you just show up, grab a drink at the bar, slide in back, and listen to music. Sometimes three, maybe four acts in one night, and it might be anything: folk, classical, crazy bouncy Eastern European brass funk. Maybe bluegrass played by a violin virtuoso, maybe four young jazzsters figuring it out. You might hear something mind-blowingly great, you might not. Stick around for the next set. You never know.

"It's more of a destination bar now," co-owner Olivier Conan says. "Less of a local bar. The neighborhood has changed so much." That's true. Back in 2002, when he and Vincent Douglas opened Barbès, South Slope was home to more artists and musicians. As the neighborhood fancied up, the creatives were priced out, but Barbès keeps that weird old Brooklyn spirit alive with its eclectic lineup of world music and cheap drinks. The place draws two different crowds who love it for different reasons.

First there's the bar crowd: they love the front part of Barbès for the after-work and weekend vibe, the good Scotch, twelve beers on tap, and the daily happy hour. It's a lively scene in the late afternoon and early evening, a crowd of twentysomethings and middle-agers, some from the neighborhood, some from, well, all over the world. Up front feels like a good cocktail party: lots of drinking and talking, and when the bands go on in back, you can hear the music plenty well, without worrying about annoying other listeners if you feel like chatting and yukking it up.

It's a different story in the back. "It's so small," Conan says, "and the music is presented in a very unpretentious way, but it's a *listening room*. There's no talking. It's an amazing place to see a string quartet." You pass through a doorway draped with a heavy black curtain, and you're in another environment. It's all about the music (or, on occasion, the spoken word) in that little fifteen-by-fifteen-foot space. You go back there to listen, probably standing up, since there are only a few seats and a couple tables. It might get packed, and in the summer it can get *steamy*, but that's all part of the fun. Just have a cold drink on hand and you'll be fine. During each set someone weaves through the crowd with a tip jar, and you're

IN THE BACK ROOM YOU CAN'T HELP BUT NOTICE A BOXY SIGN HANGING *on the* WALL THAT READS *HOTEL D'ORSAY*. IT'S BEEN AT BARBÈS SINCE SOMEONE FOUND IT IN A TRASH HEAP *in* 2001, TOSSED OUT AFTER IT WAS USED AS A PROP *in the* 2002 MURDER FLICK *PEOPLE I KNOW*, WHICH WAS FILMED IN NEW YORK AND STARRED AL PACINO *and* KIM BASINGER. DIDN'T SEE IT? "IT GOT PANNED," AS CONAN PUTS IT.

encouraged to kick in ten bucks or so. Open up your wallet, because where else in New York can you see musicians playing their hearts out, practically in your lap, for only ten bucks? It all goes to the musicians, too. Beyond the drinks they sell during performances, Barbès makes no money off the music. As musicians themselves (they play groovy-funky-exuberant South American *chicha* music in a band called Chicha Libre), the owners have great respect for performers.

"We have a worldwide reputation as a music venue," Conan says. "Musicians like it here." That's not an exaggeration. Very few small venues in New York—hell, in the *world*—could ever hope to draw the talent Barbès does. Norah Jones played here. And Madeleine Peyroux. And Bill Frisell, and a hundred equally talented musicians you've probably never even heard of. At Barbès you can see magnificent artists from all over the world playing almost any kind of music you can think of, every night, right there at the corner of Ninth and Sixth. Roll the dice, go to Barbès, and see what you see.

WHEN TO GO	I'd recommend what Conan calls "the segue from lazy café to music venue." This would mean arriving before the first act goes on, which might be five in the afternoon, might be eight at night, so you'll want to check Barbès's online calendar first. Just show up a couple of hours before that first act and cop a seat out in the front room. Enjoy the relaxed vibe of the place, maybe with friends, or just you and a book. The musicians show up, lugging their gear back to the music room, then their fans come, and the crowd grows, the energy builds, and the conversation bubbles. Pretty soon the first set starts and the whole atmosphere shifts, like the moment of kickoff in a football stadium. Head to the back and dive into the show close-up, or stay in front and listen from where you're perched. You win either way.
	Happy hour: Daily before 7 p.m., $3 off cocktails and $1 off beers.
WHERE TO SIT	If you're there for music, just stand against the wall to the left of the door in the back room. Want the bar experience? Go for the banquette seating in the very front, to the right as you walk in. There, you're in the heart of the cocktail party, with a place to sit and a window that looks out on Ninth Street.
WHAT TO DRINK	Start with a Chilcano de Pisco, the national drink of Peru, something "you can't get just anywhere," as Conan says. Follow that up with the Ultima Palabra, an unusual riff on the already-unusual Last Word cocktail, made with mezcal in place of gin.

Chilcano de Pisco

2 ounces Macchu Pisco brandy
½ ounce fresh lemon juice
1 or 2 dashes of Angostura bitters
About 4 ounces Fentimans ginger
  beer

Combine all the ingredients in a highball glass filled with ice and stir. Garnish with a lemon wedge. *Salud!*

Ultima Palabra

¾ ounce Vida mezcal
¾ ounce green Chartreuse
¾ ounce Luxardo maraschino
  liqueur
¾ ounce fresh lime juice

Combine all the ingredients with ice in a cocktail shaker. Shake well and strain into a chilled coupe glass.

Subway: The F and G trains stop at Brooklyn's 7th Avenue station, just a block up Ninth Street from Barbès.

The name Barbès comes from the Barbès-Rochechouart Métro station on the north side of Paris. Conan and Douglas, originally from France, love that vibrant neighborhood, loaded with Arab and African immigrants, outdoor markets, and restaurants. "It's the 'anti-*Amélie*' Paris," says Conan, referencing the cutesy 2001 romantic comedy set in the Montmartre neighborhood. As a bonus, the name has "bar" right in it ("so it's easy to remember," Conan says), *and* gives a nod to 376 Ninth Street's previous incarnation as a barbershop.

The back room of Barbès is visible from the front through a large interior window, and on its sill sits—usually—a bust of José Gregoria Hernández, MD (1864–1919), a Venezuelan physician, cult figure, and possible candidate for sainthood in the Catholic Church. He's sort of the patron saint of Barbès already. In 2011 the bust was stolen by a young man described as a "hipster," but was ultimately returned. He was a good man, Dr. Hernández, known for treating the poor, free of charge.

BED-VYNE BREW

370 Tompkins Avenue (at Putnam Avenue)   BEDFORD-STUYVESANT, BROOKLYN
bed-vyne.com · *347-915-1080*

"THIS USED TO BE DO-OR-DIE BED-STUY, RIGHT HERE," one of the owners, Michael Brooks, told me as we sat on the small deck facing Tompkins Avenue, referring to the Bedford-Stuyvesant neighborhood's rough past. "In the late seventies, that was a liquor store–bar across the street, and this"—he jerked his thumb toward the Bed-Vyne building—"was a 'fuck hotel'!" My, my, how things have changed. "It's no longer 'do-or-die,'" said co-owner Rotimi Akinnuoye, who owns 370 Tompkins, where Brew occupies the ground floor. "Now it's 'rent-or-buy.'"

I heard about Bed-Vyne Brew from a longtime local patron. This charming little bar sits on a quiet corner, next door to its sister bottle-shop, Bed-Vyne Wine & Spirits (Brooks and Akinnuoye co-own it and a few other bars as well, along with partners Peter Medford and Ayo Akinnuoye). Kitty-corner from an old bodega, Bed-Vyne is at the crossroads of Tompkins and Putnam Avenues, and at a figurative crossroads of this place and time.

Forget about the hot-sheet hotels of yesteryear; Bed-Stuy is a hot tourist hub now, with local home-owners Airbnb'ing spare rooms to visitors from all over the world, who often find their way to Bed-Vyne. It's a cool, youngish, diverse scene with friendly, positive energy. A lot of that starts with the welcoming bartenders (Chanel Woods Love and Norie Manigault, when I've visited), who know how to host. They also know their beers and wines, and will help guide you to something you'll enjoy and maybe have never heard of. This is a big bonus, as often even excellent beer bars have no good wine options, making it tough to hang out there with someone who's not into beer.

Our first visit was in late August, a hot time in old New York, when a lot of people leave town. It was quiet and slow at the crossroads. We took our drinks (a Great South Bay blood orange pale ale for me and a glass of the house white for my wife) onto the deck facing Putnam Avenue and met a couple of guys and their friendly little mutt. Some regulars hung out on the deck facing Tompkins, talking and enjoying a smoke. The post-church crowd drifted by in their Sunday best (Brooks told me he once counted twenty-one churches on Tompkins alone within a few blocks of Bed-Vyne), and we settled into the sweet, shady afternoon.

LOOK CAREFULLY ABOVE THE FRONT DOOR *and* YOU'LL
SEE THE GHOSTLY REMINDER *of a* PREVIOUS
BUSINESS THAT ONCE OCCUPIED 370 TOMPKINS:
LA TABLE EXQUISITE, A FRENCH BAKERY.

BED-VYNE BREW

WHEN TO GO

Want to feel the neighborhood and just take it easy? Go on a weekend afternoon. Want to meet people, enjoy some music, and/or dance? Visit Bed-Vyne Brew most any evening when the DJs take over. There's never a cover.

Happy hour: Monday to Friday, 4 to 8 p.m. $1 off all beer and wine.

WHERE TO SIT

The deck out front. It's like having your own stoop in this classic Brooklyn brownstone neighborhood.

WHAT TO DRINK

You're at a place with "brew" in the name, so try one of their beers. With ten rotating drafts to choose from (mostly U.S. craft beers, including regional favorites like Barrier Brewing, Captain Lawrence, and Empire) and around twenty bottles, you'll find something to love. For round two (or if beer's not your thing), have a glass of wine. These guys own a well-stocked bottle store next door, so you'll have some fine options (including their private labels), mostly from Italy, France, Spain, and Portugal.

HOW TO GET THERE

Subway: The A and C trains stop at Nostrand Avenue, about a ten-minute walk from Bed-Vyne Brew. The G train stops at Bedford-Nostrand, about fifteen minutes away.

WHAT ELSE?

Bed-Vyne Brew is an event-centric place. There's always something going on: music, wine and beer tastings, community fund-raisers, release parties. "There's never a slow night here," says Brooks. At one event in 2013, Nelson Mandela's daughter Maki and granddaughter Tukwini came from South Africa to the corner of Putnam and Tompkins to launch their House of Mandela wines. "Nelson Mandela loved wine," Akinnuoye told me. Nelson Mandela: statesman, freedom fighter, oenophile. Who knew?

Music at Bed-Vyne is a thing. Most nights they'll have a DJ working the booth in back, by all the empty kegs. Motown Mondays feature "exclusive remixes, originals, and close relatives of your favorite Motown songs." On other nights they spin and remix reggae, hip-hop, funk, soul ("classic *and* future"), African, and more. The crowd moves, and people spill out onto the decks. It's sexy.

BERG'N

899 Bergen Street (between Classon and Franklin Avenues) CROWN HEIGHTS, BROOKLYN
bergn.com · *718-857-2337*

FINDING A SPRAWLING, WIDE-OPEN spot like Berg'n in this town is like finding a twenty-dollar bill on a subway platform. In theory it can happen, but does it? Berg'n is vast. Expansive. There's room to move, no line at the door to get in, and light everywhere. It pours in from the skylight and the two full-size glass-paned garage doors that open to the front. In the words of Jen Watson, Berg'n general manager: "You can roll in with six to eight friends, lock down a table, and roll all afternoon." Amen, sister.

It's a social hub for all kinds of people from the thriving neighborhoods around it: Crown Heights, Bed-Stuy, Clinton Hill, Prospect Heights, and beyond. Folks flock here to hang with friends, hold meetings, throw birthday parties, get married, and dig into sprawling, drawn-out brunches. People regularly meet up at Berg'n for Ping-Pong matches, CSA produce pickup, Trivia Tuesdays, Coloring Club ("Drink and draw the night away"), rescue-dog runway shows, and just good old happy hour. Community, defined in a hundred ways, happens here.

Cofounder Jonathan Butler says, "We're a legit gathering space and a workspace for a lot of people." Plenty *do* work here, setting up their laptops for the day and getting it done. Watson says, "It's great to get out of a small New York apartment and into a large space to work. Alone, but *together*."

Community, the heart and soul of Berg'n, is mainly why people love it, but the other features put it over the top. With its long, sleek wooden picnic table seating, bright walls, and high ceilings, plus twelve taps and a full bar, it can feel like a rowdy postmodern beer hall. Berg'n boasts a full coffee bar, two pinball machines, a courtyard, a giant projection TV screen, and dynamite food. *Oh*, the food: four separate kiosks housing a rotation of food vendors, each one a favorite from Brooklyn's wildly popular eating extravaganza Smorgasburg (cofounded by Butler and Eric Demby), which showcases more than one hundred local purveyors of inventive chow every Saturday and Sunday.

With the packs of friends, multifamily groups, and couples I saw at their Sunday brunch, Berg'n reminded me of a picnic area at the state park near my hometown: spacious and open to everyone, a mix of all ages and types of people, all enjoying the communal space, eating, drinking, laughing, and being human. Sure, it's got walls and a roof, but Berg'n creates an outdoor, parklike feel and a place to be part of something big: life.

Saturday brunch is a high-energy social scene that's great for a group. For a more low-key vibe, Watson suggests showing up at Berg'n midweek in the late morning and hanging out to "watch it evolve." She says, "Have coffee, lunch, beer, a snack, a cocktail, a proper dinner. You can use it however you want."

Happy hour: Tuesday to Friday, 4 to 7 p.m. $2 off select drafts; $4 bottles and cans.

Butler likes the spot left of the elbow at the twenty-seat 1930s-era bar they found in a salvage yard in Scranton, Pennsylvania. "Good surveying spot," he says. If you're with a group, grab a table right in the middle of the room and enjoy the vibe.

AT ONE TIME THE BUILDING WAS A STUDEBAKER AUTOMOBILE SERVICE STATION.
TAKE A LOOK at the EXTERIOR ON THE DEAN STREET SIDE
AND YOU'LL SEE THAT OLD SCRIPT-Y STUDEBAKER LOGO NEAR THE TOP.

WHAT TO DRINK

Start with one of their righteous draft beers, many of them local. The lineup changes week to week and includes some "one-off, super-esoteric" selections, as bartender Shelley Kensler told me one afternoon. You'll find things like Grizacca, a dry-hopped saison from Maine's Oxbow Brewing, Von Trapp pilsner from Vermont, and Fully Frothed Imperial IPA from Brooklyn's own Other Half. Don't like beer? Have a biodynamic wine—*"No hangovers!"* says Kensler. Or order a Manhattan. For a beer hall, these guys have a strong cocktail program.

HOUSE RECIPE

Manhattan

2 ounces Old Overholt rye
1 ounce Carpano Antica
Formula red vermouth
2 dashes of Angostura bitters

Stir all the ingredients with ice in a mixing glass. Strain and serve in a chilled coupe glass. Garnish with a lemon peel.

HOW TO GET THERE

Subway: Take the A or C train to the Franklin Avenue stop, an eight-minute walk away.

WHAT ELSE?

When I first heard the name Berg'n (or, more accurately, saw it), I was a little annoyed. I assumed (wrongly) that it was just part of that cutesy trend to spell business names goofily, like Lyft, Tumblr, Hooli, and for that matter, the "hip" rebranding of all Brooklyn as BKLYN. Well, the actual story is interesting, with historical integrity. Look around the place and you'll see some old metal signs that say BERG'N in a no-nonsense sans serif font. Turns out these once adorned a subway stop, long unused, on the GG line, which stopped at Bergen and Smith Streets, not far due west of Berg'n. The IND subway line mounted these signs on the girders, which were apparently just too darn thin to fit that enormously fat second E. Jonathan Butler found a bunch of those signs on eBay, bought them up, and the rest is history.

BOHEMIAN HALL AND BEER GARDEN

29-19 Twenty-fourth Avenue (at Twenty-ninth Street)   ASTORIA, QUEENS
bohemianhall.com   ·   *718-274-4925*

I'D HEARD ABOUT THE BOHEMIAN HALL AND BEER GARDEN in Queens for years before going there. *Years.* People I knew and trusted raved about it, but my first thought was always *"Queens?"* and my second was *"Beer garden? Great. I've been to beer gardens in Munich, but this being New York, there'll be two thousand drunken, sunburnt twenty-two-year-olds, shellacked in beer, screaming like a cage full of beagles slowly being lowered into an enormous deep fryer. Whee."* (Ol' Man Grumpus, that's me.)

Well, I was wrong. I admit it. And I'm glad I was, because visiting the Bohemian Hall is a damned delight, well worth the trip to Astoria. And I stand behind this statement even after traveling over an hour from Brooklyn some summer weekends, when train service is often a nightmare due to seemingly endless subway repairs and, the alternative, a cab or car service, is slow (and pricey). I *earned* that first beer, and boy, I was happy I made the effort.

Walk through that gate on a summer afternoon and you'll be dazzled. You leave the grime and stink of the city behind, and head into the beer garden of Eden! The space is huge, like a state park—with real, towering *trees*, not those shrubs you find in the little backyard patio bars of Manhattan. Just listen to the breeze rustle the leaves and you'll start to cool off. In a minute you're at a shaded picnic table, surrounded by groups of youngish friends, middle-agers, oldsters, lunch dates, dominoes players, and families with kids. Dozens of people—hundreds! All happy, de-stressified, and far from the harsh realities of summer in the city.

BHBG has an outdoor stage the size of a small garage for music (at a volume that's conducive to conversation, in my experience), a SWAT team of friendly, competent servers, and five or so large-screen TVs mounted here and there around the beer garden's perimeter, showing sports (baseball, soccer, NASCAR, Olympics), the volume generally low.

The place courses with wholesome, outdoor social energy. That's the point of beer gardens: they're clean, well-lit places to drink. They channel that Central European idea of family togetherness, Mom and Dad and their friends and relatives enjoying beers in a convivial, kid-friendly environment. Family time—with *suds!* Bohemian Hall continues this tradition, and everyone's welcome till nine at night, when the over-twenty-one-only curfew kicks in.

Beer gardens got their start in Germany, but this place is steeped in the beer, food, and traditions of Bohemia. (For those of you who might benefit from a geography lesson, the former lands of Bohemia

IN 2000 VÁCLAV HAVEL, THEN PRESIDENT
of the CZECH REPUBLIC, VISITED BOHEMIAN HALL,
HOSTED A PRESS CONFERENCE, AND PLANTED A LIME TREE,
WHICH STILL GROWS *in the* BEER GARDEN TODAY.

BOHEMIAN HALL AND BEER GARDEN

are now, more or less, the westernmost part of the Czech Republic, bordering Germany, Poland, and Austria.) Bohemian culture lives on among the people who historically came from that region and—luckily for us—here at Bohemian Hall.

This is why the biggest sellers at BHBG aren't the German beers Hofbräu and Spaten (good as they are), but Czech/Bohemian brews like Pilsner Urquell (founded in 1842, in Pilsen), Czechvar (1785, in Budweis), and Staropramen (Prague's finest since 1869). Then you've got traditional Bohemian food like *klobása, halušky, utopenec, svíčková*, and, of course, good old *tlačenka*. Not familiar dishes? We're talking hearty European soul food here: sausages, gnocchi, more sausages, slow-roasted beef and pork, served up with potatoes, sauerkraut, and Czech-style dumplings. Man, they're all wonderful and—would you believe it?—pair well with beer. The Bohemians knew what they were doing in the food-and-beverage department.

But that's just *part* of Bohemian Hall. The beer garden is managed by the Bohemian Citizens' Benevolent Society of Astoria, which dates back to 1892. The cornerstone of the brick-and-mortar hall itself, next to the beer garden, was laid in 1910. Take a look inside. It's well-built and sprawling, and has a bit of an ethnic social club vibe, with guys watching soccer (and, sure, the Mets) at the bar upstairs and enough room in the social hall downstairs to host one hell of a wedding reception.

But for us non-Bohemians, the huddled masses yearning to be quenched, there's the beer garden—trees, breeze, music, and friends. A little bit of paradise behind a wall in Queens.

BOHEMIAN HALL IS HOME *to* NEW YORK'S OLDEST OPERATIONAL BEER GARDEN. AT ONE TIME THERE WERE MORE THAN EIGHT HUNDRED THROUGHOUT NYC, THREE IN ASTORIA ALONE. *IN* 2001 THE HALL MADE THE NATIONAL REGISTER *of* HISTORIC PLACES.

WHEN TO GO	Saturday and Sunday afternoons, in warm weather. As evening falls, a younger crowd shows up to party and the line to get in grows long. Bonus: Live music on summer weekends. (Check bohemianhall.com to see who's playing and when.) *Happy hour: Monday to Friday, 5 to 7 p.m. $4 half-liter mugs of draft beer and $14 pitchers.*
WHERE TO SIT	Pretty much anywhere in the beer garden. Some tables are in the sun, some in the shade. Sit near the stage if you want to be close to the music, at the periphery if you don't. Park in front of a big screen if you're into the game, far away if you're not. Choose your own adventure. You might end up sharing a table with other folks, which is cool. (It's a beer garden. Be social.) They're big picnic tables, pushed together in long rows, so there's generally plenty of elbow room. There are also a few standing bistro tables here and there, if you want a spot to rest your beers and hang out with a big group of friends. You generally get table service at most of the seats, but you can grab your own beers and food from the outdoor service stands, too, if you're hanging at a standing table or just sort of floating around the beer garden.
WHAT TO DRINK	Most popular: beer, of course. Have a Pilsner Urquell, the Bohemian granddaddy of the most popular style of beer in the world, pilsner. Next: enjoy a Czechvar lager, the *other* Budweiser!
HOW TO GET THERE	Subway: The N and W trains stop at Astoria Boulevard, about a six-minute walk from Bohemian Hall.
WHAT ELSE?	Why's the neighborhood called Astoria, by the way? Interesting story. Before it was ever part of New York City, it was just a nice little part of Queens County called Hallett's Cove. In the early eighteen hundreds, local boosters tried to lure investment from New York's John Jacob Astor, then the richest man in America, so they renamed the village Astoria. That's just sad, but it gets worse. Astor, who summered in upper Manhattan, could look right across the East River at Astoria, yet never even set foot in it, and only invested a measly five hundred dollars of his forty-million-dollar fortune in his namesake town. Still, they kept the name Astoria. Ain't that a kick in the pants?

BRONX ALEHOUSE

216 West 238th Street (at John M. Collins Place) KINGSBRIDGE, THE BRONX
bronxalehouse.com · *718-601-0204*

THE BRONX ALEHOUSE KNOWS WHAT IT'S DOING. This place is up-to-date, functional, fresh, and professional, backed up with solid business fundamentals and a true love *for* and understanding *of* beer. If you like a classic beer bar and have a real appreciation for the modern craft of beer, then you'll love the Alehouse.

A lot of that is thanks to James Langstine, a visionary sort who opened the Alehouse in 2009. Craft beer was not yet a thing in the Bronx back then, and a lot of neighborhood beer aficionados had no place to go. And that's a bummer. I mean, the Bronx is home to 1.5 million people, many of them dreadfully thirsty and cursed with good taste. Since 2009, they've had a home. A fine one, too.

The Alehouse is what you want in a proper beer bar: a really long bar, lots of wood, some exposed brick, a few TVs, a lively, friendly vibe, tables on the sidewalk out front, and—so important—an affable, competent, beer-savvy staff. You walk in and you just *know* that this place has it together.

The Alehouse manages a kind of old-school beer-bar feel, with modern touches like damn fine food and flat-screen beer menus designed by Digital Pour above the bar providing easy-to-read, real-time stats on every beer in house, including price, serving size, glassware, ABV, percentage of each keg remaining, and what's "tapping soon." It's a remarkably clever use of technology, and "much easier and safer than the chalkboard we used to have," Langstine points out. "Climbing on a busy, often wet, backbar right in front of the taps was getting pretty messy."

The Alehouse's sixteen draft lines and one cask might seem skimpy for a beer bar, but there's a well-considered reason for that number. "We thought it was the perfect amount of variety, but small enough to move everything quickly," Langstine explains. "Nothing is worse than walking into a place, seeing one hundred lines, and knowing at least half of them barely move. So we try to use about half of our lines to cover the most popular styles and the other half to get things that are often more unique, limited, seasonal, et cetera. We try to make it so that there's something for the craft beer novice and the total beer geek, and everybody in between."

It's just another example of the place's attention to detail, and that gets me back to the basic philosophy behind the Bronx Alehouse. "We wanted to have a place where you could get a great beer, eat great food, watch the game with friends, bring a date, be by yourself, or have a party," Langstine says. "So since 2009, this place has become all of those things to the regulars. My two favorite things to hear are, 'The neighborhood really needed a place like this,' and, 'I moved to this neighborhood because of this place.'"

BRONXTOBERFEST HAPPENS EVERY YEAR AT THE
ALEHOUSE *in* EARLY OCTOBER. BE THERE.

WHEN <u>TO</u> GO	After work on a weekday. "It's when you see the most regulars, many of whom are now friends because of this pit stop they make on their way home," says Langstine. "It's busy, but not too crowded to find a space, usually." *Happy hour: Daily, 11:30 a.m. to 7 p.m. $1 off all beers (draft and bottles/cans).*
WHERE <u>TO</u> SIT	Where the front of the bar meets the wall, to the left as you walk in the front door. "You have your own corner to lean on," says Langstine. "Plenty of space, easy access to the bartender even when it's packed, and the best view of the door to see everyone when they come in."
WHAT <u>TO</u> DRINK	First, may I recommend a beer? Specifically, an IPA. "The newest IPAs from American craft brewers are what most people are going after, and there's a new one on tap every couple of days," says Langstine. "We have mostly local ones from breweries like Gun Hill (in the Bronx), Barrier (Oceanside, New York), SingleCut (Queens), Grimm (Brooklyn), et cetera." Next, go with a yeasty German Hefeweizen. "We always keep a classic Hefeweizen on tap, and it's one of the few styles that American craft breweries can't seem to do as well as a traditional German brewer," Langstine explains. "So while our menu tends to be ninety percent American beer, you'll always find we'll have one of the classics like Weihenstephan, Ayinger, Paulaner, or Erdinger."
HOW <u>TO</u> GET THERE	Subway: The 1 train stops at 238th Street, half a block away.
WHAT ELSE?	A little more about the "digital chalkboard" above the bar. I love it, and I'm surprised you don't see them around New York more often, but that might change soon. Digital Pour designed the system a few years ago, and describes it on their website as "a robust customer-facing digital menu driven by a powerful back-end system that integrates with point of sale, website, mobile apps, and social media." Bronx Alehouse manager Dave Lindsey discovered it while on a "beercation" in Portland, Oregon, and brought the idea back to New York.

The Alehouse adopted it, making it the first bar in New York to use the system. All the stats on the board—how much of the keg is left (in real time), next keg on deck, new kegs as they're tapped, ABV content of each beer—link automatically to the Alehouse's website, so that's always up-to-date, too. In addition, the board displays social media check-ins by customers and integrates with Twitter, Facebook, and Instagram. The system is highly customizable and looks great. You gotta admit, it beats the hell out of a smudgy, hard-to-update, filthy, difficult-to-read chalkboard.

THE Alehouse is what you want IN A proper beer bar: a really long bar, lots of wood, some exposed brick, a few TVs, a lively, friendly vibe, tables ON THE sidewalk out front, and—so important—an affable, competent, beer-savvy staff. You walk in AND you just know that this place has it together.

THE BRONX BEER HALL

(Inside the Arthur Avenue Retail Market)

2344 Arthur Avenue (between East 186th Street and Crescent Avenue)   BELMONT, THE BRONX
thebronxbeerhall.com   ·   347-396-0555

THE BRONX BEER HALL IS A VERY NEW YORK KIND OF PLACE. First of all, it's in the middle of a mostly Italian marketplace, in the middle of a traditionally Italian neighborhood. Then there's the origin story: you've got these two Puerto Rican brothers, go-getters working with a local, semi-famous food guy to shake things up and bring a good idea to fruition, changing something old and good into something even better. It's Bronxy. It's New Yorky. It's a hell of a fun place to visit.

Owners Paul and Anthony Ramirez are not just *from* the Bronx, they're huge advocates *for* the Bronx. In 2007 they started a company to promote their home borough and its businesses, music acts, and image. In 2011 they opened a pop-up store in the Arthur Avenue Retail Market, a collection of shops, vendors, makers, and grocers in the Bronx's Little Italy. There they successfully sold Bronx T-shirts, Bronx hats, Bronx hoodies, Bronx everything, and it got them thinking, "You know what'd be cool? A place to drink good New York–made beer right here in the middle of the market, with all this excellent food, and all these great people."

The guys found a champion in David Greco, one of the food kings of the market. Greco's eggplant parmigiana smacked down Bobby Flay's on Flay's *Throwdown!* show in 2010, and with him vouching for the pair, the Brothers Ramirez got the Bronx Beer Hall off the ground in February 2013. It breathed new life into that great old marketplace, and brought in folks who ended up not just drinking, but shopping, eating, and meeting others there in the heart of the neighborhood. "We're helping bring the Arthur Avenue Market into the twenty-first century," Paul says. "The more attention we bring to the Beer Hall, the more attention we bring to the market. They see what we're doing here, and people in the Bronx are even inspired to open their *own* Bronx businesses."

Here's what it's like: you walk into the market, through French doors, and once inside, you're immediately engulfed by it all. It's a big, open carnival of ten different shops, with all their different counters and signs and flags and customers young and old, and food, food, *food*. Cheese galore, hundreds of colorful boxes of pasta, bottles of olive oil in dozens of shapes and sizes, and the occasional whole lamb or goat head, traditional favorites from the butcher. Aromas come at you like a commuter rush: fresh bread, fresh produce, fresh mozzarella, fresh sausages. Stuff for sale: over here you've got hand-rolled cigars, over there you've got wiseguy T-shirts with *Godfather* jokes, and over there, that

KARAOKE NIGHTS ARE KIND OF A BIG DEAL AT <u>THE</u> BRONX BEER HALL,
WHERE YOU'RE INVITED to "COME SING WITH US in a COMPLETELY JUDGMENT-FREE ZONE—
JUST LIKE PLANET FITNESS." THEY'RE USUALLY on TUESDAY NIGHTS AT EIGHT,
AFTER THE MARKET CLOSES AT FIVE and the OTHER VENDORS HAVE SHUT DOWN.

guy? That guy's making sandwiches to order as big as Sylvester Stallone's head, I swear ta God. Big as his freakin' *head*.

It's an opera of sounds bouncing around under that twenty-foot ceiling: carts rolling and rumbling, cash registers beeping and bipping, people calling out orders over high counters, and behind it all, strains of doo-wop, Sinatra, and old-school soul.

In the middle of this delicious chaos, there's an oasis. Right in the heart of the market, under the skylights, you'll find a freestanding, conventional-looking wooden bar that seats about ten, and a dozen or so long wooden tables with benches, the seating for a food court with an embarrassment of culinary riches in every direction: hot Sicilian-style pizza, spicy soppressata heros, fresh cannoli. And then there's that cold, local beer.

On our first visit to the Beer Hall, we dropped in on the postgame football crowd from nearby Fordham University, scored seats at the bar, and ordered up a Bronx Banner golden ale (me) and a nice glass of red wine recommended by the bartender (she). We chatted with a couple of recently minted Fordham alumni and watched a college football game on the two screens above the bar. The wife noticed all the great-looking chow that several other customers at the Beer Hall were digging into, so she went a-shopping, coming back from Mike's Deli a few minutes later with the antipasto plate of the decade: a mound of cheeses, tomatoes, cured meats, bread, olives, and peppers, all for about fifteen bucks. It was a *yuge*, generous mountain of food, perfect with wine and beer, and way more than we could've finished ourselves, so we shared with our neighbors at the bar.

We could have just ordered from the Bronx Beer Hall's menu—it's all sourced from within the market—but you're welcome to walk around and choose your own adventure from any of the market's vendors, and I think that's part of the fun. Get some cheese over here. Get some prosciutto over there. Need an espresso? *Check*. Gelato? *Right there*. It's fun. It's social. It's very, very Bronx.

WHEN <u>TO</u> GO

Saturday afternoon, when the retail market is in high gear and full of shoppers, some of them taking a break at the beer hall, having a bite to eat, hanging out with the Fordhammers. "Saturdays are so much fun," says Anthony. "You've got the communal tables, the bar, and you can meet people."

Happy hour: Monday to Friday, 4 to 7 p.m. $2 off all pints, $5 glasses of wine, and special prices on pitchers.

WHERE TO SIT

According to Paul, the bar is where you want to be during the day, but in the evening (especially if you're with a group), go for table five, near Mike's Deli and Peter's Meat Market. It's good shopping action/people watching, *and* you can conveniently wrangle your dinner just steps from your seat after gawking at folks buying all that tempting chow.

WHAT TO DRINK

Beer. "What I would recommend," Anthony says, "is, talk to the bartenders for suggestions. Ask for samples. That's what they're there for." They have six beers on tap, almost exclusively from New York breweries. Go for a flight of four, sip away, then pick your favorite and order a pint, or even a whole pitcher. Another solid option is wine—surprising at a beer hall, but it makes sense when you're surrounded by all that great Italian food to pair with it. The BBH has a fine selection of wines from New York State and all over the world, including (of course) Italy.

HOW TO GET THERE

Subway: The B and D trains stop at the Fordham Road station, about a fifteen-minute walk (or a short cab ride) from the Arthur Avenue Retail Market. Of course, when you're going deep into the Bronx, a car is an option worth considering. It can be a long train ride, and on weekends, the subway can be complicated, due to repair work and limited weekend service.

WHAT ELSE?

The Arthur Avenue Retail Market anchors what Bronxites call "New York's *real* Little Italy," the Belmont neighborhood. Back in the thirties, Arthur Avenue and other commercial strips around town were crowded with individual pushcart vendors selling all sorts of edibles: vegetables, fish, cheese, meat, prepared food, etc. New York mayor Fiorello La Guardia wanted to clean up the streets, modernize the city, and move the vendors inside, so he built a few indoor markets around NYC like the one on Arthur Avenue, which opened in 1940. Others include the Moore Street Market (1941) in Brooklyn, La Marqueta (1936) in East Harlem, and the Essex Street Market (1940) on Manhattan's Lower East Side.

BROOKLYN ICE HOUSE

318 Van Brunt Street (at Pioneer Street)   RED HOOK, BROOKLYN
718-222-1865

dive \dīv\ *n*

1. A well-worn, unglamorous bar, often serving a cheap, simple selection of
    drinks to a regular clientele.
    —*Urbandictionary.com,* 2017

2. A disreputable bar or pub. Individual bars may be considered to be
    sinister, of poor upkeep, or even a detriment to the community.
    —*Wikipedia.org,* 2017

THERE ARE A COUPLE OF radically different ways to interpret the word "dive" as it applies to bars. For the record, you won't be reading about what I would call a *bad* dive (see definition 2) in this book. Bad dives often stink like dog kennels, and give off the energy of a man with stage IV bladder cancer.

And if the Brooklyn Ice House is a dive, it's certainly a *good* dive (see definition 1). A *damn fine* dive. From spring to fall, the door to the backyard is often wide open, so when you enter, you're greeted with a clean breeze, that golden-brown-barbecue aroma, and usually some pretty dang good music. "We use Pandora, so each bartender creates their own tight stations," the bartender Eddie told me on a weekday afternoon. You'll hear an unlikely-but-seamless blend of reggae and new wave pop one afternoon, then later that week maybe a mix of deep sixties soul, or Dwight Yoakam + nineties grunge + Dolly Parton + Salt-N-Pepa. (Good thing, this constant stream of well-chosen music, considering the USE AT YOUR OWN RISK sign taped to the jukebox.) The bartenders spice up the atmosphere like the kitchen does the food. And man, that remarkable little kitchen adds so much to an Ice House visit.

"Newcomers are shocked by the food, how decent it is," says owner Trevor Budd, a surfer/snowboarder dude originally from Australia, now a fortyish Brooklyn dad. "Decent" is an understatement. Their chili is one of the best I've had in New York, a deep, dark, all-meat-no-beans Texas stew, slightly sweetened and thickened with corn flour. It satisfies the soul, and so do the onion rings, sweet potato fries, and their surprisingly inventive specials, many vegetarian-friendly. Didn't see *that* coming from an Aussie-Texan dive, didja, mate?

The Ice House's scruffy barbecue roadhouse vibe is partly inspired by Budd's wife, Elaine, who's from San Antonio. When you're parked at the bar over a shot, beer, and bowl of chili, you'll feel like you're hanging with the regulars in a local joint, a mile outside of town in the Lone Star State. If you want some sun and fresh air, great. Head out back and enjoy the spacious yard with its picnic tables, shaggy ivy walls, and mural of a bipedal quisling pig, cheerfully tending a smoky Weber grill while drinking a Porkslap beer.

"People are surprised we *have* a backyard," Budd says. "If that door in back is closed, you wouldn't even know." Don't judge a bar by its cover. That sweet backyard is just another bonus you wouldn't expect from the crusty exterior of the Brooklyn Ice House.

THE FRONT DOOR'S LARGE GLASS PANEL *is* ALMOST COMPLETELY PLASTERED OVER *by* STICKERS (FOR BEERS, BARS, BANDS, *and* STUFF I CAN'T DISCERN). I ASKED BUDD WHY. "IT WAS TOO BRIGHT IN HERE, SO WE STARTED PUTTIN' UP STICKERS." *OKAY.* (IF YOU GOT ONE TO ADD, *STICK IT.*)

WHEN TO VISIT	Saturday and Sunday afternoons, when it's lively but not so busy you can't get a seat. *Happy hours: Monday to Friday, noon to 8 p.m.: $1 off all drinks (except the beer/shot specials). Saturday and Sunday, noon to 3 p.m.: $2 for cans of PBR and bottles of Miller High Life.*
WHERE TO SIT	In the backyard when the weather is good, or the round table by the front door (good for up to six or seven folks) if it isn't. You win either way. Budd keeps the backyard open late, thanks to "pretty cool neighbors" who don't complain about some boisterous conversation.

Start with a shot and a beer, the perfect roadhouse drink. The Ice House serves combos like the Stevedore (a can of Pabst and a shot of Evan Williams whiskey) and the Highbeam (a bottle of Miller High Life and a shot of Jim Beam), and the price won't break the bank. Next drink: go deeper into the beer list (they've got dozens of bottles in stock, including some pretty obscure treats), or how about a Moscow Mule made with Tito's Texas vodka? They stock all them copper mule mugs for a reason, son.

HOUSE RECIPE

Ice House Moscow Mule

2 ounces Tito's vodka
¾ ounce fresh lime juice
3 or 4 ounces Regatta
    ginger beer

Combine the vodka and lime juice in a large glass (or a copper mug, if you happen to have one) loaded with ice, and stir. Top with ginger beer and garnish with a lime wedge.

HOW <u>TO</u>
GET THERE

It's Red Hook, a remote part of Brooklyn without any direct subway lines. You're best off taking a car or riding your bike, but if you're patient, you can catch the B61 bus from Brooklyn's Borough Hall, where several subway lines converge. You can also take the Wall Street Pier 11 South Brooklyn ferry to the Atlantic Basin in Red Hook, a couple of blocks west of the Ice House.

WHAT ELSE?

Notice the small brass plaque mounted low on the corner of the bar to the left as you walk in. In October 2012, Hurricane Sandy plowed into New York City, shoving an already very high tide right up into—and through—many low-lying waterfront areas. Red Hook got walloped, and the Ice House suffered a couple feet of standing water, now marked by that plaque. The remarkable thing is that despite the devastation, the bar opened just a few days later, a gathering spot for wiped-out neighbors and friends. We hung out there one night with our buddy Sorgatz shortly after Sandy, observing bartender Maddie Bouchard loaning her apartment key to neighbors who needed a hot shower. That's the night I fell in love with the Ice House.

BROOKLYN INN

148 Hoyt Street (at Bergen Street)   BOERUM HILL, BROOKLYN
718-522-2525

"WHEN WE TOOK OVER THE BUSINESS, we had one mantra: let's be smart enough not to fuck it up. It's legendary for a reason." So says Jason Furlani, manager since 2007, on the responsibility of buying the venerable Brooklyn Inn, one of the oldest bars in a borough that values its old bars. "What is amazing is that, throughout time, everyone saw the value in the space itself," notes Furlani. "There have been minor additions and improvements over the years, but the one thing that is consistent is that no one fucked it up. The room itself is sacrosanct."

When you walk into the Brooklyn Inn, it's almost like you're entering a church. The twenty-five-foot ceilings soar, as does the intricately carved, almost altar-like mahogany backbar. Stained glass glistens, tin cherubs watch over you, and woody gargoyles grimace, high above the bartender.

Since 1885 congregants have assembled here, taking communion (in glasses only; nary a wafer is served) and connecting with each other. "It's the people," bartender Heather Clinton tells me when I ask her what she loves about the place. Regulars are revered here, but first-timers are equally welcome. "It's typically a steady mix of regulars and newbies," says Furlani.

The mood of this neighborhood institution runs the gamut from sacred to profane. On a Saturday afternoon the place can be as quiet as a law library, every patron reading, writing, or waiting for a friend. Five hours later it's absolutely raucous, like a roaring, whiskey-fueled 1958 cocktail party at George Plimpton's pad, friends and strangers pressed shoulder to shoulder, banging elbows, talking, drinking, howling, yawping.

"Saturday nights are the wild-card night. That's our 'anything can happen time,'" Furlani says. "It can be a shit-show of young, entitled asshats, or a wedding party [as in: the *entire* wedding] will show up, or three birthday parties will pile in like a clown car." But Sundays at the Brooklyn Inn are special in a different, *much* quieter way. Maybe it's the inn's churchy atmosphere. When light pours in all those big corner windows, it's transcendent. Furlani puts it this way: "We're a harbor in the calm waters of routine and a port in the storm of life. We do the same thing every day, and we welcome both newcomers and regulars with open arms. Long as they don't rock the boat. It's hallowed ground, something to be both respected and revered."

WHEN <u>TO</u> GO	I like Friday, Saturday, or Sunday afternoons, when the crowd is sparse and the whole room glows with magical light that highlights the relief of the bar's carvings, not to mention all that stained glass. For a rowdier time, stop in for a Friday or Saturday (anything can happen) night.
WHERE <u>TO</u> SIT	"I could tell you that, but then I'd have to kill you," Furlani says. "Only because the regulars would show up on my lawn with torches and pitchforks. I have a family to think about." My personal favorite: the leftmost seat at the front end of the bar, which has a great view of both the room and the street outside. Come winter, it's conveniently located near the radiator. Just watch out for those regulars with their torches and pitchforks . . .
WHAT <u>TO</u> DRINK	Start with a Guinness. Their system mixes nitrogen and CO_2 for the perfect pint. "One of the best outside of Ireland—perfectly calibrated, perfectly cold, and always fresh," according to Clinton. Then order a shot to go with that Guinness. Pours are heavy and prices are light.
HOW <u>TO</u> GET THERE	Take the G or the F train to Brooklyn's Bergen Street stop, then walk a block east to Hoyt. You can transfer to the G (or take a short walk) from the A and C at Hoyt-Schermerhorn.
WHAT ELSE?	In the back room that holds the pool table, you'll see several defunct doorbell-like buzzers above the wainscoting. Decades ago, when the Brooklyn Inn was a restaurant, diners in back would summon waiters with a push of these buttons, like attendant call buttons on airplanes. People still love to press them, looking around like naughty little kids to see if anything will happen.

NOTICE the STAINED-GLASS PANELS that ADORN THE MAIN ROOM, INCLUDING A STATELY "AZ" FROM 1885: THE INITIALS of the ORIGINAL OWNER, ANTON ZEINER, A PILLAR of the LOCAL GERMAN-AMERICAN COMMUNITY.

CORNER BISTRO

331 West Fourth Street (at Jane Street)   WEST VILLAGE, MANHATTAN
cornerbistrony.com   ·   *212-242-9502*

I'D BEEN TOLD ABOUT CORNER BISTRO before I even moved to New York—countless times, usually by younger friends who loved to go a-boozin' in the West Village. And they always, *always* sang the praises—operatically, even—of Corner Bistro's burgers. *The burgers! The burgers! OH MY GOD, the burgers! They're hot! They're juicy! They're reasonably priced! They're served on PAPER FREAKING PLATES, hot and fresh when you really need them: late, after a night of drinking! Starch and fat! Starch and fat! STARCH and FAT! The Burgers the Burgers the Burgers!*

Kind of like that.

And I wrote it off as happy drunk talk (well, they were sober at the time, but essentially it was talk inspired by *past* happy drunkenness), so I didn't really give much credence to their praise, and didn't make it to Corner Bistro until years after moving to New York City. But eventually I got there.

It was snowing that night, coming down hard. My wife, Colleen, and I were meeting our friends, Tuten and The Gauche, for drinks after work. I'd suggested Corner Bistro, just in case anybody was hungry. And yes, I wanted to finally try that burger.

We met on a Friday evening at around six, prime time, just as the place was filling up. A lot of folks stood in line along the left side of the front barroom, waiting for tables in the back dining area. Forget that. I wanted to be up front at the bar, where the action is.

We nabbed a spot near the bar's elbow, by the front window and out of the line of traffic, which gets hairy on Friday nights. We ordered three beers and a whiskey sour (for Colleen), hung out, and watched the snow fall. Our beers came in hefty glass mugs, ribbed on the sides, with handles. I love those mugs. They make even the crappiest beer taste 35 percent better.

We drank and talked, laughed and drank, and the snow kept floating down, steadily, and we were cozy as cats on the hearth there in the Bistro, perhaps warmed, if only subliminally, by the red neon of the iconic Corner Bistro sign outside. The snow fell. And fell. And *fell*, and settled in fresh, clean mounds on the corner of Jane and Fourth. Time passed, snow drifted, and traffic thinned out. We watched intrepid cabs drop people off, and they'd climb awkwardly over the rising snowbanks and down onto the sidewalks, laughing.

The Bistro's sign glowed in the flurry, snow settling on its neon pipes, timeless and nostalgic, like a wintry Hopper painting, minus the sad, listless woman whose face you can't quite see. To the contrary, every face I saw was happy as hell. We were all tucked into our little corner of the West Village, sheltered from the storm with friends and beer on a Friday night in one of the world's most legendary

CORNER BISTRO COOKS ITS CHUNKY BEEF BURGERS in a MULTISTORY *SALAMANDER* OVEN (A BIG BROILER). WHY BROIL A BURGER? WELL, FIRST OF ALL, IT'S FAST, AND WHEN YOU'RE CRANKING OUT HUNDREDS of BURGERS A NIGHT LIKE CORNER BISTRO DOES, TIME IS MONEY. SECOND, THE BURGER DOESN'T LOSE AS MUCH OF ITS JUICES AS IT MIGHT WHEN GRIDDLED or FLAME-GRILLED. THIRD, IT'S HEALTHIER: IT'S NOT COOKED in a BUNCH OF GREASE and FAT.

neighborhoods. Everyone laughing, drinking, feeling warm and loved. I fell for Corner Bistro right then and there, and I hadn't had burger-one yet.

That changed in short order. We got fries and burgers, along with more drinks, and dug into those juicy mothers the second they came to us, still pipin' hot.

The evening and snow drifted on, and we drank more, but we had burgers for ballast, so we didn't capsize. We weathered the storm, steady as she goes, sharing the experience with everyone else hunkered down in the Bistro, safe and warm in the hold of our cozy ship.

Oh, and the burger was good—moist and hot and it'll do the trick when you need it. I consider it a bonus, a sidebar, a *feature* of the Corner Bistro. The good old-fashioned feel of the place is what really makes this hangout special. That, and the fact that there's always a lively crowd.

The location is sweet, too, deep in the West Village, where streets veer eccentrically off the NYC grid any damn way they please: at angles, bending north, bending south. The Bistro's a perfect place to settle in and let New York roll on by as you watch it from the window of the bar. Sit there and just be. And of course, try the burger. Even my vegetarian wife has fallen off the wagon for it a couple of times, so they're doing something right.

WHEN TO GO	Right after work on a weekday. Enjoy the crowd. Have a couple of drinks, like a civilized human being, then order your burger and stay for dinner.
WHERE TO SIT	The ledge in the front window, facing the corner of Jane and Fourth, a wonderful perch from which to watch the West Village, the crowds, the traffic, and the weather.
WHAT TO DRINK	Get a beer in one of those thick, heavy glass mugs with a handle. They're the best. They have eight taps to choose from, so start off with something on the lighter side. How about a McSorley's ale, a nod to another great good place just a mile to the east? Next drink: Well, you're going to need *some*thing to wash that burger down, aren't you? Let's go with a classic: a cold mug of Yuengling lager, made in Pottsville, Pennsylvania, since 1829, making it the oldest operating brewing company in the United States.
HOW TO GET THERE	Subway: The A, C, E, and L trains all stop at 14th Street–8th Avenue, and the 1, 2, and 3 trains stop at 14th Street–7th Avenue, all within a couple of blocks of the Bistro.

CRONIN AND PHELAN'S

38-14 Broadway (between Thirty-eighth and Steinway Streets)   ASTORIA, QUEENS
croninandphelans.com   ·   *718-545-8999*

IT'S A SOCIAL PLACE, CRONIN AND PHELAN'S. Classic Queens, opened in 1902 by Thomas Cronin and Pat Phelan. It's unpretentious, a place where you can bring the wife and kids for dinner or hang out with the boys and watch the game at the bar, which is to your right as you walk in. You'll often find menfolk aplenty hanging out and watching the Mets or Jets there, while on the left side of the room you'll see the dining area, with the mix: moms, dads, grandparents, kids. Everybody eating and drinking and enjoying one another's company.

The owner is Mike Peacock, an Irishman who came to the United States back in 1968. He's been at Cronin and Phelan's since 1990, and plays the role of tavern host with grace and easy enjoyment. It's guys like Peacock who make a pub or tavern what it is. The personality of a place often comes from the top down, and in Queens, with dozens and dozens of Irish taverns and pubs, personality is a huge differentiator. You've got your old-man pubs, your young-guy pubs, your yuppie pubs, your family pubs, and your Archie Bunker pubs. All kinds of pubs in Queens.

Cronin and Phelan's has, for an Irish place, a beer-hall sort of vibe, with an assortment of patrons (singles, couples, families, old, young, men, women) and a surprisingly extensive menu.

"I love this place," says Roger, a Queens neighbor from nearby Sunnyside. "The beer's cold, the whiskey's good deal, and you can eat like a king for next to nothin', compared to the rest of New York." And eat you can. The Irish fare is what you want. C & P's best sellers are the chicken, shepherd's pie, and bangers and mash. It's a solid, all-purpose pub and grill, where you can hang out, have a drink and a filling meal at a fair price, and get a feel for this part of Astoria, another New York neighborhood in the middle of transition, from those old Archie Bunkerish pubs to glossy clubs, restaurants, and cocktail bars. But the pubs were the social backbone of Queens neighborhoods like Astoria, and though several have closed, the many that are still left are well worth a visit, for a taste of another era and some damn fine, rib-stickin' food, too.

LONGTIME BARTENDER DAVE CREMIN *is* KNOWN TO WORK A LITTLE MAGIC *at the* BAR. THE KIND WITH PLAYING CARDS AND SUCH. *SLEIGHT OF HAND.* IF YOU'RE LUCKY, YOU CAN CATCH HIM DOING HIS THING DURING HIS EVENING SHIFTS.

WHEN TO GO	Friday evenings. Head to the right and have a seat at the bar for a round. Then hop over to the left side of the room for dinner in the dining area. It's the best of both worlds.
WHERE TO SIT	The end of the bar toward the front door. Easy bartender access, and a great view of the whole bar.
WHAT TO DRINK	Guinness. Jameson. Let's not complicate this.
HOW TO GET THERE	Subway: The E, M, and R trains stop at Steinway Street, just one block away. Queens caveat: on weekends—due to repairs, construction, and acts of the good lord—you'll need to double-check the train schedules. Don't be a fool. Don't make the same mistakes I've made. (*Damn you, Google Maps!*) One Saturday I started out to Queens from Brooklyn on my tried-and-true, one-transfer subway route, only to be confounded from the get-go. One train not running, alternate line undergoing repairs, my trusty transfer route closed for weekend tunnel work, a harried MTA employee shouting last-minute reroutes right there on a platform in deep Manhattan. A suggested route taking me well out of my way just to catch *another* train that would (hopefully) cross the East River and out to Queens. Download the MTA's Transit app and hope for the best. *You've been warned*, boyo. *You've been warned. . . .*
WHAT ELSE?	Cronin and Phelan's sits half a block off Steinway Street, named for the family that built its second piano factory just up the road in 1871 (the first was located in Manhattan). In addition to the factory, the Steinways established a little community for their employees nearby, complete with brick row houses, a park, a library, and a school. In the eighteen hundreds, around twelve hundred employees called "Steinway Village" home. As long as you're in the neighborhood, why not check it out? And Steinway offers factory tours on Tuesdays, nearly year-round (but not in July and August). Book in advance—space is limited (info@steinway.com or call 718-721-2600).

Sitting at the Bar vs. Sitting at a Table

A guy walks into a bar. Then he must make a choice: sit at a table or sit at the bar. I used to be a sit-at-a-table guy, but now I'm a devotee of bellying up to the bar. Here's why.

If you're feeling social, then sitting at the bar is the natural choice. There are more people, and a professional with practiced social skills right in front of you at all times. Many of us work at home these days, spending too much time alone, and we need an injection of human interaction. After all, we're tribal beasts. Sitting at the bar can be your salvation, brother, especially as a lunch break (if you've got a lot of work to do, you can just order coffee or a Coke), or at 5:01 p.m. for a much-deserved happy hour. Even if you've come with a friend, sitting at the bar will up your social quotient. But sometimes you come to a place alone, and want to *be* alone. You can do that at the bar, too: just bring a book or poke away at your phone.

Parking it at the bar has other advantages beyond the social. The view, for instance. Sitting at the bar raises you up above table level, so you can scope out the whole place from your lofty perch. There's typically a mirror on the back of the bar, too, so you can see everything going on behind you. I prefer the corner-most bar seat (picture the lower-right part of the letter *L*), with the wall at my back, for the best sightseeing.

Another benefit of sitting at the bar is better service. Bartenders are generally pretty competent characters, the front-of-house top dogs. They *have* to be (or *should* be) more courteous to customers at the bar—you're right there, in front of them. They can't easily disappear on you or pretend they don't see you. Having this essential player nearby and at your service eliminates the middleman (the server), allowing you to get your drinks and food faster.

The bartender can also serve as a sort of concierge, assisting when you have special needs like a phone charger, catching your game on some obscure cable channel, or a recommendation for your next stop of the night. Granted, you shouldn't expect this sort of help during a three-deep happy hour crush at P. J. McGillicutty's on the night before Thanksgiving. But even during an insanely busy happy hour, you'll often get better service sitting at the bar than anywhere else in the joint.

However, there's a time and a place to sit at a table, too. Maybe you want to share a fine meal, and companionable conversation, with a date or close friend, and enjoy it at the standard, time-tested dining altitude of thirty inches off the floor. Or perhaps you want some private time, in which case, *might monsieur prefer a booth?* Or, for the best of both worlds, sit at one of the tall, big-boy tables in the bar section, if they're available.

THE EAR INN

326 Spring Street (at Greenwich Street)   SOHO, MANHATTAN
earinn.com   ·   *212-226-9060*

FOR MOST OF ITS HISTORY, New York wasn't the kind of city to romanticize its past. There simply wasn't time. There was *money* to make! *Business* to do! A *city* to build, dammit! And so buildings—and sometimes whole blocks—were torn down to make way for new development, changing the character of entire neighborhoods. But somehow, the scrappy little building at 326 Spring Street remains, a survivor of New York's long-gone past.

The place was built in 1817 by James Brown, aide to George Washington during the American Revolution and a freeman of color. The two-story wooden structure stood just five feet from the Hudson River until landfill a few years later pushed the shoreline one block westward. Unless *perhaps* it was built in the late 1770s using charred timber salvaged from the Great Fire of 1776. Or, you know, *maybe* around 1790. Facts are soft, records are missing, and for its first couple of centuries, New York didn't really care too much about yesterday anyway.

Talk to the owner of the Ear, Martin Sheridan, and he'll tell you what he knows about its history. The Irishman says recent excavations of the foundation unearthed heaps of broken Champagne bottles and oyster shells, thought to have been tossed by Dutch picnickers enjoying breaks from the crowded hustle of New Amsterdam (population six thousand), a mile to the south. Historical business records indicate that 326 Spring was Brown's tobacco warehouse in 1817, the same year records show alcohol was first sold there. By the 1890s, Irishman Thomas Cloke owned the place, brewing beer and bottling whiskey on-site and serving it up to the mariners and longshoremen who worked on or along the Hudson.

Eventually the shipping business moved away, causing jobs to dry up and the bustling neighborhood to slow down. Then 326 Spring became a speakeasy during Prohibition and a hangout for homeless men and underemployed dockworkers during the Great Depression. Around that time, New York's master builder, Robert Moses, started his massive *slum clearances* and renewal of the city, which changed everything. Well, *almost* everything. Old buildings were razed left and right, but in the sixties, New York's Landmarks Preservation Commission was established, and designated 326 Spring as an official landmark—"a modest example of an early nineteenth century Federal house"—thus sparing it from obliteration.

The building was saved, but business was iffy. The only patrons of the bar were fading old dockworkers, many drinking away their pensions. But there was hope! Rip Hayman, a student from Columbia University seeking downtown adventure, moved into the upstairs apartment in 1973. His roommate

Sari Dienes, an artist, was one of many creative types who rediscovered downtown Manhattan during New York's financial nadir. In 1977 the roommates, along with bartender Paco Underhill, bought the bar, then known as the Green Door (because, well, the door was green) from then-owner Harry Jacobs.

A renaissance followed, bringing music, art events, poetry, and life back to the joint, and in 1979 Jerry Walker and Sheridan, patrons of what was by then called the Ear Inn, bought it, "saving it from a committee of owners who did everything they could to discourage business," as Sheridan cheekily puts it. (The place was christened the Ear Inn, after the music magazine published on the second floor, when Hayman used some black paint to mask the rounded edges of the letter *B* in the neon BAR sign above the door, a quick-and-dirty end run around the Landmarks Preservation Commission's red tape regarding facade changes.)

An artsy crowd took the place of the old dockworkers at the bar, followed by money, as yuppies colonized the neighborhood in the eighties and nineties. Tourists began stopping in and enjoyed the Ear about as much as the regulars did. Business picked up and remains steady, consisting of a blend of neighbors and visitors to this site near the intersection of the West Village, Tribeca, and Soho, a weird corner of Manhattan with no precise neighborhood moniker. Lower Greenwich? The South Village? West Soho? You tell me.

The Ear remains a link to post–Revolutionary War New York, when the city's population was smaller than today's in Appleton, Wisconsin, and the waves of the Hudson River pounded a few feet from the front door. Go in, order a beer or a bite, and soak it up.

WHEN TO GO	At lunch you'll find locals taking a break from work, reading or chatting with the bartender and one another. Friends gather after work on weekdays for a lively happy hour. On Sunday evenings the place fills up when the house jazz band, the EarRegulars, do their thing. *Happy hour: Monday to Thursday, 5 to 7 p.m. $1 off all drinks.*
WHERE TO SIT	Mr. Sheridan says his favorite is the corner seat, by the wall closest to the front window. Why? "It's the most profitable seat in the house." It also boasts the best light, and a full view of the room and everyone at the bar.
WHAT TO DRINK	Order a pint of Guinness; they pour it *proper* here. Also good: the St. Summer, a quenchy, refreshing cocktail (see recipe).

THE OLDEST PART *of the* EAR INN IS HELD TOGETHER *with* WOODEN PEGS, NOT NAILS. THE BENEFIT, ESPECIALLY IN NEW YORK JUST STEPS FROM THE HUDSON, WAS THAT AS TEMPERATURE AND HUMIDITY FLUCTUATED, PEGS WOULD EXPAND AND CONTRACT IN CONCERT *with the* WOODEN BOARDS THEY WERE HOLDING TOGETHER, ENSURING A SOLID JOINT REGARDLESS.

HOUSE RECIPE

The St. Summer

3 ounces Tito's vodka
⅔ ounce St-Germain
elderflower liqueur
Splash of fresh lime juice

Stir all the ingredients in a mixing glass with ice. Strain and serve up in a chilled martini glass with a lemon twist.

HOW TO GET THERE

The Ear is a little out of the way from any subway line. It's not *actually* in the West Village, nor *really* part of Soho, and it's *near*, but not actually *in*, Tribeca. That means you'll have to hoof it a bit from the nearest subway stops: Houston (1), Canal (1), or Spring (C, E), each about six blocks away.

WHAT ELSE?

"See the history of New York City just lookin' over the bar," says Sheridan, pointing to shelves and walls full of artifacts like old two-tone whiskey jugs, vintage policemen's uniform patches, nautical-looking carved figurines, various caps worn by the world's sailors decades ago, mugs and bells and barometers, and an impressive glass jar that once held a whole heap of something called "Foley Cathartic Tablets." Take a gander at the ceiling while you're at it, if only to see the horrifyingly graphic vintage poster of *Hardacre's Temperance Map Illustrating the Effect of Alcoholic Drinks and Narcotics on the Human System*, which includes vivid, full-color illustrations of a "hob-nail liver" and the blotchy red-brown stomach lining in the "last stages of delirium tremens" that looks like the background of a painting by Hieronymus Bosch. Then order another Guinness or three. *Fast.*

FARRELL'S BAR & GRILL

215 Prospect Park West (at Fifteenth Street)   WINDSOR TERRACE, BROOKLYN
718-788-8779

WALKING INTO FARRELL'S IS LIKE WALKING INTO A CLUBHOUSE, at least when the regulars crowd the bar, most all of them men, many of them cop and fireman types with fiercely blue eyes. But it's all right. Belly up to the bar. Don't bother looking for a stool. There aren't many at Farrell's, and they're for the older guys anyway. Get up there and order the freshest thirty-two ounces of Budweiser you'll get outside of St. Louis, served cold, in a Styrofoam behemoth of a cup—called a container—to keep it cold. Listen to the guys at the bar bullshitting each other. Talk to the bartender. Talk to the guys. Have another container of suds.

The first time I went to Farrell's I was a little intimidated. I'm not Irish, I'm not a local, and I look more like a professor of Nerdological Studies than a cop. But I *had* to go to Farrell's. It's legendary. The bar played a major role in newsman/screenwriter Pete Hamill's memoir, *A Drinking Life*, which I loved. Hamill's dad, Billy, drank at Farrell's, and Pete knocked back a few there, too. It's like that at Farrell's, generations of a family drinking at the same bar (there's soda for the kids).

Regular Pat Halpin's Windsor Terrace roots go back to his great-grandparents. "Farrell's is the town hall of the neighborhood," he tells me. "It's in the Irish tradition of the pub being *the* neighborhood place, where everybody gathers, gets the news, finds a job, a place to rent, a house to buy." Halpin says Windsor Terrace, at the southwestern end of Brooklyn's huge Prospect Park, is like a small town, its own "little village with a lot of city workers and an Irish perspective." It does feel that way, though the neighborhood, like all of New York, is changing, with people moving in from all over the city and the rest of the world. But Farrell's isn't changing . . . much. A new floor here, a new sign there, but the place is basically what it's been since it opened in 1933, right after Prohibition: a no-frills place for the guys— and, since 1980, women—of Windsor Terrace to do it their way. And that means more than drinking out of those big white cups. It means taking care of the neighborhood.

Owner and Bartender Hall of Famer Jimmy Houlihan started at Farrell's in 1965. "Hooley" (his nickname is spelled like the Irish slang term for a wild party) is legendary for aiding local people and organizations in need. He's helped fund neighbors' medical co-pays, hosted neighborhood reunions to raise money for local schools, and set up a scholarship in memory of firefighter and part-time Farrell's bartender Vinnie Brunton, whom Windsor Terrace lost on 9/11. In 1995 Hooley and the Farrell's community organized three hundred volunteers to paint local Holy Name School's thirty-three classrooms, an enormous job they did in one day.

Jimmy Houlihan is that kind of old-school local barman, and Farrell's is that kind of old-school local bar. "It's what you do for the neighborhood," he says. "People take care of people."

Belly up *to the* bar. Don't bother looking for a stool. There aren't many *at* Farrell's, and they're for the older guys anyway. Get up there and order the freshest thirty-two ounces *of* Budweiser you'll get outside of St. Louis . . .

WHEN TO GO	End of the workday, after five. Bonus: Houlihan works the bar Thursday and Friday evenings.
WHERE TO SIT	Sit? No, you *stand* at the bar at Farrell's. You go up to the bar like a man and you stand.
WHAT TO DRINK	First: a thirty-two-ounce container of Bud. Next: a thirty-two-ounce container of Bud *Light*. Show some restraint.
HOW TO GET THERE	Subway: The F and G trains stop less than a block away, at 15th Street–Prospect Park.
WHAT ELSE?	True story (or "total bullshit," depending on who you ask): It's a late night in the early seventies, and Farrell's has yet to serve a woman a drink at the bar. Ladies and kids in the back room, men up front. Officially. So in comes the writer Pete Hamill—Pete who grew up in the neighborhood and drank at Farrell's like his dad and his brother Denis and all the other Hamills—with this beautiful redhead, the actress Shirley MacLaine, his date for the night. Well, she wants a beer, and she walks right up to the bar and orders one. And gets it. First woman to be served at the bar at Farrell's. "It was late, like ten minutes to four in the morning," Hooley recalls. "The young guys were workin' the bar that night, and they just served her. It was no big deal." A few years later, in 1980, the ban was lifted and women were officially allowed at the bar.

I gotta tell you one more thing about that beer, because, yes, I love a craft beer, but I also love a cold macrobrew now and again, and this Bud they serve at Farrell's is truly, remarkably, damn good. That's partly because it's so fresh, thanks to the volume they sell, and the lines are cleaned every two weeks, but it's also because it's served so cold, and a Bud has *got* to be cold to taste good. The bartender Mike showed me the trick: it's the "jockey box" tap system. He lifted the stainless steel plate on the bar above the beer taps (Bud, Bud Light, and Stella Artois). The steel box underneath was packed with fresh ice, and that ice hugged the three coiled hoses that fed the beer from the refrigerated kegs below to the taps above. Every inch of that beer is kept ice-cold, and those famous Styrofoam cups—briefly banned by the city but allowed again, thanks to new recycling technology—*keep it* cold in your hot little mitts.

TAKE A LOOK at FARRELL'S CLASSIC NEON SIGN OUT FRONT. IT GLOWS with FOUR DIFFERENT COLORS, AND IT *LOOKS* LIKE IT DATES to the TIME FARRELL'S OPENED IN THE THIRTIES. YEAH, BUT IT'S A REPRODUCTION. THE ORIGINAL, MADE IN ABOUT 1935, FELL TO THE SIDEWALK in the CHRISTMAS BLIZZARD OF 2010. IT WAS BUSTED UP BADLY ENOUGH TO MERIT REPLACEMENT, BUT THEY TOOK ONE SIDE of the ORIGINAL SIGN and RESTORED IT WELL ENOUGH TO WORK AS AN INDOOR DECORATION. IT HANGS by the BIG SCREEN in the BACK ROOM (FORMERLY THE DINING ROOM, WHERE LADIES AND KIDS WERE ALLOWED, USING THE ENTRANCE on FIFTEENTH STREET).

FLAGSHIP
BREWING COMPANY

40 Minthorne Street (at Bay Street)   TOMPKINSVILLE, STATEN ISLAND
flagshipbrewery.nyc   ·   *718-448-5284*

THE FIRST TIME WE WENT TO THE FLAGSHIP BREWING COMPANY'S tasting room, we were driven out by a bunch of little kids. I didn't see *that* coming.

Seriously. We showed up at Flagship midafternoon on a Sunday, opened the front doors, and were blown away by a gale-force military-style drum solo. Turns out a group of young percussionists had an event there that day, a "drum student roundup," and they were really banging it out. I mean LOUD. After the initial shock, I realized, *hey, this is actually pretty cool.* Here's a brewery with a dedicated space that the folks of Staten Island can use as a sort of community center, but better, because there's plenty of fresh beer for Mom and Dad as they smile, drink, socialize, and video their kids beating the living hell out of those drums.

Flagship Brewing Company opened in the Tompkinsville neighborhood of Staten Island in 2014, the vision of local boys Jay Sykes, John Gordon, and Matthew McGinley. "People truly enjoy the beers we make," says Sykes, "*and* the authentic feel our place gives off. It's a place that's growing with the neighborhood, where the people of the community can come to talk about the issues that affect it, while enjoying an unforgettable beer."

Neighborhood issues include "major projects that will change the face of our shoreline forever. But to me," Sykes says, "the beating heart of this change is the small businesses and people of this community. So we are changing, but staying true to what we really are."

And what they are is part of New York City's brewing renaissance, and that's going strong, especially since the passage of new state laws that have sparked further growth in the industry. Local folks are embracing their new local breweries—specifically the tasting rooms—as their own neighborhood bars/community centers/performance venues.

It's good to see. Adopt Flagship as your own. Stop by in the middle of the day and check out what's happening. It might be a completely tame afternoon, with a few folks sipping beer at the picnic tables throughout the airy, high-ceilinged tasting room, or it might be a peewee drumming extravaganza. Stop by at night and party with your pals or take in some local music. (Check the website first; tasting-room hours are limited and event times will, of course, vary.)

KEEP YOUR EYES PEELED *for* FLAGSHIP'S BRIGHT BLUE ROLLING-BAR BEER TRUCK. IT'S A FORMER BREAD DELIVERY VEHICLE, TRICKED OUT *with* REFRIGERATION *and* SIX TAPS. "IT WAS THE IDEA OF ONE *of our* FIRST INVESTORS," SAYS JAY SYKES. "HE WAS ADAMANT THAT WE GET ONE, *SO* ADAMANT THAT ONE DAY IT JUST SHOWED UP OUTSIDE THE BREWERY. AFTER TAKING ONE LOOK AT IT WE KNEW HE WAS RIGHT. WE BRING IT TO EVERY FESTIVAL *or* OFF-SITE EVENT."

WHEN TO GO

"If you want to chill out and talk with the guys from the brewery about the beers, then I would say Friday afternoon," Sykes says. "We usually all get off work and have a pint before starting the weekend. Saturdays we offer tours in the afternoon and music at night." You might get to meet the man behind these fine suds, brewmaster Patrick Morse.

WHERE TO SIT

With luck you can snag the recliner in Flagship's "living room," up on the stage. When it's not being used by musicians, the space is set up with couches, lounge chairs, a coffee table, and a fireplace.

WHAT TO DRINK

Start with a flight, choosing four five-ounce pours of the seven or eight beers they have on tap at the time. Sykes says, "To really get a good idea of what our brewery is all about, try our IPA, lager, and the Kill Van Kölsch," so you might want to work those three into your four picks. Enjoy your flight, and then get a full pint of your favorite.

HOW TO GET THERE

The Staten Island Railway (SIR) stops in Tompkinsville, and Flagship is literally a one-minute walk down Minthorne from the station. You can hop on the SIR at the St. George Terminal of the Staten Island Ferry, which runs year-round from Manhattan's southern shore. The ferry is free and a great way to see Miss Liberty. It'll also give you a feel for New York's geography, including the vast harbor that made the city what it is today. By car, you can pay the hefty toll and take the Verrazano-Narrows Bridge.

WHAT ELSE?

This neighborhood brewery was started by three legit Staten Island neighborhood guys. Founders Sykes, McGinley, and Gordon grew up next door to each other in the island's West Brighton neighborhood, just a couple of miles from Flagship, and even attended the same grammar and high schools.

Look at the Flagship logo. The orange is the very same color as the Staten Island Ferry. Look carefully and you'll notice a tiny buck's head on the left side, a nod to Staten Island's native deer population. Oh, and that big guy with the antlers on the wall behind Flagship's bar? That's an elk, not a deer. Just so you know.

FORT DEFIANCE

365 Van Brunt Street (at Dikeman Street)   RED HOOK, BROOKLYN
fortdefiancebrooklyn.com   ·   *347-453-6672*

ST. JOHN FRIZELL MOVED TO BROOKLYN'S QUIET, REMOTE Red Hook neighborhood in 2003. It was even more low-key back then, a relic of Brooklyn's shipping heyday, its lack of subway lines setting the harborside neighborhood apart from the rest of the city. There were a couple of good dive bars, and the usual bodegas and bagel joints. Frizell loved Red Hook, but there was no place to get some of the staples that he—a copywriter at *Bon Appétit*—wanted, like a proper mixed drink, a nice glass of wine, a good cup of coffee. "There was nothing quite like Fort Defiance in the neighborhood back then. I waited for one to open, then finally did it myself."

He did that in 2009, and Fort Defiance, named after a Revolutionary War fort hastily constructed in Red Hook before the British invasion of Brooklyn, soon became a kind of community center where people see their neighbors, exchange news, and find roommates or a new apartment. In the morning, regulars stop by to get their coffee, tuck into biscuit egg sandwiches, and read the day's papers on old-fashioned newspaper sticks. By twelve thirty the lunch crowd rolls in—folks who work at home, local artists, tourists, and employees of the neighborhood's small independent businesses. After three the place switches over to a mellow cocktail-hour vibe as locals knock off from work, have a drink, slurp some oysters, and deconstruct their days. At five thirty the dinner menu kicks in, then after that it's nightcap time in Red Hook. Frizell says, "We're always open, so you can always stop by."

Red Hook is a tight community, and people love Frizell's place so much that he says they "get very possessive of it. They think it's their very own. They're proud of it and they bring their friends here to show it off, which is fantastic." In October 2012, Hurricane Sandy hit New York hard, and coastal, sea-level Red Hook took it on the chin. Fort Defiance got flooded and was closed for about a month, but locals pitched in and helped clean up the mess the next day, even buying "junk bond" gift certificates with half the proceeds going to the reopening effort. I understand their devotion. I've been a patron of the Fort for years, had my first "favorite bars" art show there, and now work behind the bar a couple of days a week.

Frizell knows what the place means to the neighborhood. "The fact that we're still here after the hurricane means a lot. It means we're defiant."

THE LEGENDARY CULINARY WRITER *and* BON VIVANT
CHARLES H. BAKER JR.'S PERSONAL COCKTAIL SHAKER *and* TWO GLASSES
(A GIFT *from* BAKER'S DAUGHTER) ARE PRESENTED *in a* LIGHTED
CASE MOUNTED *on the* WALL TO THE RIGHT OF THE BAR.
IN FACT, IN BAKER'S REVERED BOOK *THE GENTLEMAN'S COMPANION*,
YOU CAN SEE A PICTURE *of* THIS COCKTAIL SET,
HELD ON A TRAY BY HIS GRASS-SKIRTED DAUGHTER.

FORT DEFIANCE

WHEN <u>TO</u> GO	Fort Defiance is an "all-purpose" kind of place, as useful in the morning for coffee, breakfast, or brunch as it is late at night for after-dinner cocktails. I'd recommend a daytime visit during the week, when the mix of locals and visitors is mellower than on the weekends. But I fell in love with the place eating brunch at the bar, when it's about as busy as it ever gets. Another good option is whenever Frizell himself mans the bar. He'll make you a great cocktail and tell you the history behind it, too.

WHERE <u>TO</u> SIT

According to Frizell: "Got to be table two, the four-top banquette in the back corner. That's where all the photographers [from the press Fort Defiance has received over the years] like to shoot. Good northern light comes in through the back window and everyone looks beautiful there in the afternoon." Me, I'm a fan of seat B-twelve: end of the bar and against the wall.

WHAT <u>TO</u> DRINK

Start with a Barbados Buck in the summer, a Sazerac in the winter. And Do. Not. Miss. The Irish coffee, called "the best in the known world" by Pete Wells, restaurant critic for the *New York Times*.

HOUSE RECIPE

Barbados Buck

2 ounces El Dorado 5-year-old rum
1½ ounces ginger syrup
1 ounce fresh lime juice
3 or 4 dashes of Angostura bitters
Splash of seltzer

Shake the rum, ginger syrup, lime juice, and bitters with ice in a cocktail shaker. Strain over ice into a collins glass. Top with seltzer. Garnish with a lime wedge.

HOW <u>TO</u> GET THERE

A bit out of the way, Red Hook is tough to get to by public transportation, but that remoteness is part of its charm. There's the B61 bus, as well as the B57, but a better bet is taking a car, or, if you're feeling nautical, going by ferry. The South Brooklyn ferry goes to the Atlantic Basin, and from there it's a quick walk to Fort D. If you bike, you can lock up at a rack right out front.

WHAT ELSE?

In the early 2000s the Brooklyn-based band the National recorded a few tracks in a studio where Fort Defiance now sits.

THE GATE

321 Fifth Avenue (at Third Street) PARK SLOPE, BROOKLYN
thegatebrooklyn.com · 718-768-4329

THE GATE IS AN ARCHETYPAL NEIGHBORHOOD PUB, specializing in craft beers and located on a corner of one of Brooklyn's most Brooklyn-y neighborhoods, Park Slope. What's more, it's got an outdoor patio, and not a sorry slab of dank concrete with two crummy picnic tables, no! It's more like a mini beer garden, off to the side of the building, right there on the corner of Fifth and Third, a wide-open space with fresh air, sunshine galore, and a fine view of Washington Park across the street. Now *that*, my friends, is a patio. And that is an excellent reason to go to the Gate—preferably to meet some friends—and while away a beautiful afternoon. In its entirety.

The Gate was one of the very first bars I ever went to in Brooklyn, back in May 2002. I was visiting my beer-loving friends Washburn and the Swordfish, who lived in Brooklyn, in Prospect Heights, before we were all married and/or domesticated. Most of the visit consisted of walking around and drinking beer, and I could barely keep up with those guys. They were like beer-drinking machines, but I tried.

At some point, we trekked down Fifth Avenue in Park Slope and landed at the Gate, grabbing a table in the sun on that fine patio. I didn't want to move, partly because I was beat from walking (anyone from a car town who's ever visited New York knows what I mean), and partly because after you're a beer and a half into a situation like that—sitting in the sun with friends, surrounded by a happy crowd doing exactly the same thing—well, why would you move? The Gate is tailor-made for afternoons like that.

Owner Bobby Gagnon had a clear vision for the Gate when he and his partners, Bryan Delaney and Dave Brodrick, opened the place in 1997. "It evolved into what I wanted it to be: a community-based pub." They found the perfect location for that vision in 1996 when Delaney, stuck in traffic, happened to turn his head and see a FOR LEASE sign at 321 Fifth Avenue. He called his partners and said, "Guys, I think we found our place." That building on that corner at that time reflected the faded opulence of Park Slope, a part of Brooklyn on the verge of becoming an affluent, yuppie-parent mecca. Gagnon sensed that a renewed Park Slope would need a solid craft beer bar, and that it'd be a hit as more and more newcomers arrived with a taste (and budget) for quality brew. When he first walked into the place, he looked around and felt, "THIS is a bar space."

He was right, and inspired by the public houses of Ireland, which are open to everyone, he nailed it. "It's not a gimmick," he says. "It's not a dive. It's the *local pub*. It's a concentration of community. We take all comers here. You can meet others or sit with your own thoughts and be comfortable."

Late afternoon, to enjoy the patio, or early evening in the colder months, for a nice, quiet visit inside with the regulars. In the mood for some music? The Gate hosts semi-regular vinyl nights, listed in the events section of their website.

Happy hour: Monday to Friday, 3 to 7 p.m. $1 off well drinks, house wines, and most beers.

When the weather's right, grab any table on the patio. You can watch the river of Brooklyn traffic and pedestrians roll on by, enjoying what Gagnon calls "arguably one of the most wide-open views in town," with Washington Park right across the street.

Most popular: craft beer. Make no mistake: "It's about the beer list," Gagnon says. That's the draw, accounting for about 80 percent of the Gate's sales, and it's exactly why beer geeks seek this place out. So start with a pint. The bartenders—all beer lovers, or they wouldn't be working here—will help you pick one that suits your palate, with twenty-four taps and a bunch of special bottles to choose from. Next up: another beer, of course. Gagnon suggests "another craft beer from a different part of the spectrum."

Subway: The D, N, and R trains stop at Union Street, and the F and G stop at 4th Avenue. Either is about a ten-minute walk to the Gate.

If you look across Fifth Avenue, all the way over to the other side of Washington Park, you'll see a little old stone house known as—who'da thunk?—the Old Stone House. In August 1776, world history changed right there. A couple hundred American soldiers from Maryland held off an advancing force of two thousand British redcoats in the first major battle of the American Revolution, the Battle of Brooklyn. Most of the Marylanders were wiped out, but they fought like lions, giving George Washington and his men to the west enough time to retreat to Manhattan to fight another day. "From here to the Gowanus Canal is a Revolutionary War boneyard," says Gagnon. In fact, one of the Gate's Park Slope neighbors once found skeletal remains behind the house while digging in his backyard: "Marylander's bones," according to Gagnon.

Gemütlichkeit: That Great, Good Feeling

The best thing about the bars in this book isn't the drinks, the food, the decor, the music, or even—bless 'em—the clientele. Those are all very important, but they contribute to something bigger, something that's even greater than the sum of all those parts. It's a feeling that comes from a certain place and mood. It's a mood that comes from a certain feeling and place. It's vital to the health of our hearts and souls, and we don't even have a word for it in English. Fortunately, though, the Germans do (of course; they have a word for everything), and that word is *Gemütlichkeit* (pronounced geh-MYOOT-lik-kite). It describes a space or state of warmth, friendliness, and good cheer.

The best bars, taverns, and dives I've ever visited radiate a warm feeling of belonging and well-being. These places make you feel cozy, safe, and somehow connected, even if you don't know a soul in the room. What's better is hanging out with friends at a place that *already* glows with that fine vibe of good cheer and camaraderie. That takes things to a whole other level. *Übergemütlichkeit?*

I've felt *Gemütlichkeit* as far back as I can remember, starting at my parents' cocktail parties, where their best friends would gather in our living room, drinking and laughing, the men in coats and ties, the women, predictably, in cocktail dresses. I felt it at the Bear Lake Tavern, the local bar and grill where we'd go for dinner on occasion, on the water about a mile from our house.

I've definitely experienced this warm, inclusive feeling that comes from being among the right people in the right mood in the right environment, but I'd never heard a proper term for this rather abstract concept until I read Ray Oldenburg's classic *The Great Good Place: Cafés, Coffee Shops, Bookstores, Bars, Hair Salons, and Other Hangouts at the Heart of a Community* (Marlowe & Company, 1989), in which Oldenburg used the word *Gemütlichkeit* to explain what made German beer gardens so wonderful:

> *Inclusiveness was central to the coveted atmosphere of the lager beer garden. It was a garden in a double sense—in addition to the greenery, human relationships and goodwill were cultivated. The atmosphere in which this is accomplished most effectively has a name well understood in the German language. It is* Gemütlichkeit. *What is* Gemütlich *is warm and friendly. It is cozy and inviting.*

Oldenburg nails it. This is the element that lifts a bar to another level, from the physical to the emotional realm of excellence. It comes from attentive hosting, from proper lighting and music, from the smell of clean wood, and from the mood and attitude of the patrons. I'll take *Gemütlichkeit* over a flawless twelve-ingredient cocktail or a trendy crowd of frantically beautiful people any day.

When you find a place like this near your home, give it your business, stop by often, and add to the *Gemütlich*.

GRAND ARMY

336 State Street (at Hoyt Street)   *DOWNTOWN BROOKLYN*
grandarmybar.com · *718-422-7867*

"NO VESTS, NO TIES," Damon Boelte says. "We wanted to create a neighborhood corner bar—something for the community—with an educated bar staff but more approachable than a speakeasy."

When Grand Army co-owner/head bartender Boelte and his partners set their sights on the Downtown Brooklyn corner where the long-shuttered Victory Café coffee shop stood for years, they wanted to make something substantial. Something solid to anchor the intersection of State and Hoyt. A place where the people could gather for a proper, satisfying drink, made without pretense, gimmickry, or those whimsical, old-timey arm garters.

Boelte and Co. had a clear vision for the new bar, and it started with the name. "We wanted to reference historic Brooklyn, for sure," Boelte says. "And a name that sounded sturdy and strong. *Strong* drinks, a *sturdy* bar, a *strong* place." They found inspiration for the name a mile to the southeast: Grand Army Plaza, the main entrance to Brooklyn's Prospect Park. *Grand Army.* Named for the Grand Army of the Republic.

"I like strong stuff," Boelte tells me. "I like old cars, old motorcycles, and big old bars. We *had* to have a big, old, strong bar."

The name is solid and the venerable bar is definitely burly, but the atmosphere of Grand Army is decidedly light. That was part of the plan, too. Part of the vision.

"We wanted to create a casual, welcoming environment," Boelte explains. "Lighter and airier than the dark, old-fashioned speakeasy trend in New York at the time. More like a contemporary Brooklyn apartment or loft, with art on the walls, plants, a fireplace, and funky decor touches."

Boelte once worked as a graphic designer, and knew a thing or two about color theory. If you look closely around Grand Army, you'll start to notice the color blue. A deep, solid blue. In the logo, on the menus, the napkins, the matchbooks. "Blue is a cool color," Boelte says. "And cool colors make you slow down and *chill the fuck out.*"

It works. The place feels good—easy to settle into and accessible. Time it right, and you can walk through the corner door and slide right onto a bar stool, then watch the evening unfold. There's usually a hearty surge of after-work regulars around six.

"We have a very mature clientele who know food and beverages and like to have fun," Boelte says. You'll also see a lot of young professionals at Grand Army, some "industry people" from Brooklyn's

LOOK CLOSELY *at the* BIG MIRROR BEHIND THE BAR. LIKE MANY THINGS AT GRAND ARMY, IT'S BLUE. *TINTED BLUE.* "YOU NEVER REALLY SEE A BLUE MIRROR," BOELTE SAYS. "IT'S LIKE LOOKING INTO ANOTHER *DIMENSION!*"

bars and restaurants, and a few folks who work in the courthouses nearby. Let the tide of people and conversation rise around you, as you sip your strong, sturdy drink. Drink it *all* in, the whole place. It's nice to be there.

It's a treat to watch Boelte work. He's a total pro. A good host who works fast, pays attention to detail, and makes every drink look and taste great. He's got that lanky, longhair-outlaw-cowboy look, with Willie Nelson braids dropping out from under an immaculate Stetson. Voice is deep as a well. A welcoming, enthusiastic, eccentric, seasoned, native Oklahoman.

Like a well-oiled machine, he makes a drink, then sets it on fire. Puts it down in front of a giddy young woman, already pulling out her phone and opening Instagram. He hunches slightly, looks her in the eye, and uses the deep voice, gesturing with the long fingers, all serious. "Here's what you do: 'Gram that shit, blow it out, then drink it, in that order. Don't want you getting hurt."

WHEN TO GO	"Probably Thursday evenings," says Boelte. "Thursday is the new Friday." That's a good night to see Grand Army all revved up and full of energy, but not swamped by the weekend crush. As a bonus, if you get there early—by five, shortly after they open—you'll get to enjoy the place bathed in the last remnants of daylight, before the crowd hits, and take advantage of oyster happy hour. "It's a great place to day-drink," according to Boelte._ _Happy hour: Monday to Friday, 5 to 7 p.m. $1 oysters plus specials on varying wines and beers._
WHERE TO SIT	The end of the bar, to the left as you walk in. When the place is busy, it's like being on the bank of a tidal river, watching the flow of people coming and going, yet you're just far enough out of the fray not to get swept away.
WHAT TO DRINK	Start with a classic daiquiri. When made right, they're marvelous, crowd-pleasing drinks. Far too many of us have only had those sugary, slushy travesties that give the drink a bad name. (Think Bourbon Street in New Orleans or Duval in Key West.) Grand Army restores the daiquiri's dignity in a variety of ways, using different rums and variations on sweeteners, for instance, and you're always sure to get a right-proper version from any of the bar staff.

"Finish with a Hard Start," Boelte suggests. "We make a lot of those around here." Whatever you have to eat or drink during your visit to Grand Army, this minty, herbaceous little shot-glass digestif assures you finish on a good note. It was first concocted by Boelte himself when he was bar manager at Prime Meats, in Brooklyn's nearby Carroll Gardens neighborhood.

Damon's Go-to Daiquiri

1½ ounces Caña Brava rum
½ ounce La Favorite rhum agricole blanc
¾ ounce fresh lime juice
¾ ounce simple syrup (equal parts sugar and water, stirred or shaken until the sugar dissolves completely)
1 lime wedge

Put the rums, lime juice, and simple syrup in a cocktail shaker filled with ice. Squeeze the lime wedge over it and drop it in to get all those good lime oils. Shake with mucho gusto, strain into a chilled coupe glass, and garnish with a lime wheel.

Hard Start

Combine equal parts Fernet-Branca and Branca Menta in a shot glass, knock it back fast, then smack the empty glass down on the bar with a purposeful *thunk* and say *MMM!*

Subway: The A, C, and G trains stop a block away at the Hoyt-Schermerhorn station, and the 2 and 3 trains stop three blocks away at Hoyt Street.

The special cocktails list changes every season, each time with a distinct, unusual theme, and the drinks are named accordingly. Past themes include Oklahoma state parks, political scandals, classic prom themes, black metal music, trains and railroad lines, the color pink, and *Gilmore Girls*. No matter what you order, it'll be fun. An *adventure*. And tasty. "People are surprised by how great the cocktails are for how casual the staff is," Boelte says. "You see these guys behind the bar, wearing Hawaiian shirts and Harley tees, and then you go '*SHIIIT!* These are *good drinks*, man!'"

GUN HILL BREWING COMPANY

3227 Laconia Avenue (between East Gun Hill and Boston Roads) OLINVILLE, THE BRONX
gunhillbrewing.com · 718-881-0010

WHEN DAVE LOPEZ AND KIERAN FARRELL opened the Gun Hill Brewing Company in 2014, New York City was home to all of sixteen breweries, not one of them in the Bronx. San Diego, with about 10 percent of New York's population, had eighty-four breweries at the time. Something was amiss, and these two guys decided to do something about it, in the borough most near and dear to them.

Farrell was Bronx-born and Lopez went to school there. They met playing semi-pro baseball for the New York City ThunderDogs, based out of the Bronx's Roberto Clemente State Park. Most of NYC's brewing was happening down in Brooklyn, so the guys decided to focus on finding a spot in the northern borough, where beer hadn't been brewed since the sixties. Not a bad move. Better deals were available in the Bronx, away from the feeding frenzy over trendier Brooklyn and Manhattan real estate.

Lopez, a history buff, liked the idea of using "Gun Hill" in the brewery's name. That strategic geographic bump in the Bronx played a role in the Revolutionary War when the Continental Army hauled a cannon up to the spot by way of what's now called Gun Hill Road. As luck would have it, they found the perfect location for their brewery in an old auto transmission shop, just a few yards south of that very road, proving the name they had in mind prescient.

I discovered the brewery's appeal as a hangout after donating to an online campaign that helped fund their canning operations. We stopped by on a Saturday to pick up my thank-you gift and found a hell of a nice scene at the brewery. The big garage door was open, and folks were hanging around the threshold enjoying a fine October afternoon and pints of fresh beer. The crowd inside, a happy mix of beer geeks as diverse as the Bronx itself (black, white, Hispanic, etc.), seemed at home, drinking and snacking, chatting and laughing, hollering and watching football. It felt like a tailgate party of twenty- to fiftysomethings milling about in a gigantic garage/workshop with twenty-foot ceilings.

Hanging out that afternoon, we soaked up an industrial version of that fine beer-hall feeling known in German as *Gemütlichkeit* (a space or state of warmth, friendliness, and good cheer) among people who were together to simply enjoy life, each other, and some very good beer. No attitude, no pretense, just drinking, snacking on fresh pretzels and empanadas, and being social.

New York is experiencing a brewery moment these days—new operations with tasting rooms that double as local hangouts are opening up every other month, it seems. Places like Flagship in Staten Island, Threes in Brooklyn, and SingleCut in Queens provide their neighbors with large, lively social spaces along with their singular brews. They're bringing back a version of that wonderful old German beer-hall model, open to all comers, which thrived in the United States before Prohibition. There is a brewing revolution upon us, citizens! Join the cause!

GUN HILL BREWING COMPANY *is* WHAT'S KNOWN *as* A NEW YORK STATE "FARM BREWERY." THIS MEANS THAT THEY BREW THEIR BEER USING A CERTAIN PERCENTAGE *of* INGREDIENTS GROWN AND SOURCED *in the* STATE OF NEW YORK. IN RETURN, <u>THE</u> STATE ALLOWS FARM BREWERIES CERTAIN PRIVILEGES, INCLUDING THE RIGHT TO SELL PINTS *of* BEER ON-SITE AND GROWLERS TO GO WITHOUT EXTRA RED TAPE *and* SPECIAL LICENSING FEES.

WHEN <u>TO</u> GO	Late afternoon to early evening on weekdays, when you can catch the after-work crowd enjoying the suds up front and check out the brewing process happening in the back. A warm football Saturday afternoon at Gun Hill ain't bad either, the front door rolled up revealing a modest two TVs inside, so you can keep an eye on the game but still enjoy the weather.
WHERE <u>TO</u> SIT	When the weather's right and the front garage door is open, grab a seat outside at one of their old wooden-barrel tables, enjoy some sun, and watch the crowd come and go. If you're sitting inside, grab a spot at the far right of the bar, where you can watch the brewers work in back.
WHAT <u>TO</u> DRINK	You're here at the source, so I'd recommend opening with Gun Hill's generous beer flight. Pick six beers (the bartender will help you choose from the fourteen on tap) and enjoy five-ounce pulls of each for one low price. Regardless of what you start with, be sure to save room for a Void of Light stout, a pitch-black, roasty, slightly sweet "foreign-style" stout, high in flavor with a hefty 7.9 percent alcohol content.
HOW <u>TO</u> GET THERE	Subway: The 2 and 5 trains stop at Burke Avenue, which is a ten- to fifteen-minute walk from Gun Hill Brewing. But depending on where you're coming from, it can be a fairly long trip up to the North Bronx, especially from the outer parts of Queens and Brooklyn, so you may want to just take a car, ideally one that someone else is driving. Some of these beers pack a punch.
WHAT ELSE?	The brewers at Gun Hill brainstormed with cast members of the Broadway phenomenon *Hamilton* in 2016 to develop a Revolution era–themed beer, Rise Up Rye, using that ingredient so important to colonial agriculture, rye. The *Hamilton* crew even helped brew the first batch, which was sold at the Richard Rodgers Theatre during the show's run, and at several other bars and restaurants around New York City, with part of the proceeds going to Brooklyn's Graham Wind-ham children's charities.

How to Be a Regular

Going to a bar where they know you is like going home. And it's one of the things that makes a good place a *great* good place. Being a regular offers the satisfaction of routine, ritual, and belonging. It's the difference between being a visitor and part of the family. Becoming a regular takes time, consistency, and a little effort.

First of all, you've got to pick a bar—maybe two—and choose carefully. Use your senses. How does the place feel? Pay attention when you walk in. If you don't like the vibe, scram. Why waste your time? I prefer a subtly welcoming place with good light and favorable music at medium-low volume. Noxious smells, lousy tunes, and a nasty attitude from the bartender drive me out in a big hurry. But sometimes it's a bartender who draws you in. The right bartender can make you fall in love with a place, too.

Consistency is key in becoming a regular. Go the same day and time for a few weeks. This way the same bartender will likely be working and get to know you. Establish a routine. Sit at the same spot. I recommend the bar, where the action is, not a table. Ordering the same drink is a good idea, too. Bartenders will remember you as Beefeater Martini Guy or Ms. Daiquiri. One bartender barely remembers my name, but nails the drinks my wife and I ordered the first time he served us. Go figure.

Okay, so, what do you bring to the party? In certain chatty joints, you'll talk up the bartender, maybe other patrons, too. In other places, maybe not. Use your head. Follow the lead of the locals. If the other regulars aren't your crowd or the place ain't your scene, bail. It depends on the tone of the bar. Mind your manners. Be a good guest. Engage. Use your coaster. Don't get sloppy drunk. Say please and thank you.

Ask what's good. Any unusual beers on tap or obscure whiskeys the staff likes? This sort of chattiness might not be appropriate for all bars, but again, follow the lead of the other patrons and the bartender.

Tip generously. Twenty percent is fine, and if the drinks are inexpensive (happy hour deals, cheapo beers), tip at least a buck or two per drink. Why be stingy? As Frank Sinatra said about money, "Spread it around!" It's good karma. If a free drink ever comes your way, be appreciative, tip heavily, and don't act like you expect it to happen again. It's a gift, not a given.

When you leave, say thanks and goodbye. That's just good manners. Maybe use the bartender's name *if* he or she gave it. A person likes hearing his or her name and they'll appreciate and remember you for it, but don't act like a shingle salesman, using it in every other damn sentence. That's annoying. Don't be annoying.

HARLEM TAVERN

2153 Frederick Douglass Boulevard (at 116th Street) HARLEM, MANHATTAN
harlemtavern.com · *212-866-4500*

I'VE BEEN TO A LOT OF SPORTS BARS, and I've gotta say, generally, I'm not a big fan. *However*, when we trucked up to Harlem on the first Sunday of the 2016 NFL season, I had my best sports bar experience in memory. And the place was absolutely *packed*, Jack. Where I stood, at the fifty-yard line of the long, long bar, it was literally shoulder-to-shoulder, Times-Square-on-New-Year's packed. And I got jostled . . . maybe twice. *Slightly.* More brushed than jostled, like when you exit a busy elevator, or the subway, off-peak. Both times I got a quick, *"Scuse me, bro."*

Nice crowd, only slightly more men than women, early thirties, and racially as mixed as Harlem is these days. And for a sports bar, *way* more good-natured and social than I generally see. Most people there were into the games, sure, but for fun, and as a reason to get together and see their friends. They weren't living or dying over every dumb play, gnashing their teeth like sweaty, risky-betting sports junkies. They were yelling, laughing, drinking beer, hugging. It was just plain *fun*, the way watching sports *should* be. "Every football season is like a reunion," says general manager Faith Talley. "The same faces every year. It's great."

Service was superb. Crazy-crowded as the place was, the staff was *on it:* professional, cheerful, and hustling like crazy to keep everyone well beered. One waitress (wish I'd caught her name) kept her eye on us the whole time. Though we were standing in the middle of a sea of humanity, she checked on us regularly and quickly brought us beverages when we needed them, sans hassle, sans attitude. "This is the hardest shift," she said, cool and smiley, as we gave her a good-bye/thank-you. "They keep me on all day and I'm here every week." *I love her.*

As a place to watch football, Harlem Tavern is top-notch. The main room is enormous, with high ceilings, two dozen tables, and sixteen seats at the bar. Huge doors open wide during mild weather, bringing in fresh air, breeze, and light. The place is done up in a contemporary, middle-of-the-road style with wagon-wheel-size Edison bulb chandeliers, square wooden tables, and exposed-brick walls sporting a mother lode of TVs, which are fully leveraged on football Sundays.

Each screen had a sign beneath it, indicating the roster of games, early and late, that would be shown on that particular TV. Every NFL game was covered somewhere in the room, with the New York teams commandeering the big pull-down screens behind the bar. With each screen dedicated to specific games, the crowd subdivided around the teams they wanted to watch, so over by *that* TV you'd have all the

Service was superb. Crazy-crowded *as the* place was, the staff was *on it*: professional, cheerful, and hustling like crazy to keep everyone well beered.

HARLEM TAVERN

Tampa Bay and Atlanta fans, while all the Lions and Colts fans would hang out by *that other* TV. The loudest sub-crowd was the Philadelphia Eagles fans. It's always rowdy in Philadelphia.

Out front was a completely different story. Though there were a couple of TVs in the huge beer garden, people weren't there for football, but for food. Out there, the crowd brunched with a vengeance, and nearly every seat at every table and picnic table was filled. Among the mix were locals, tourists, post-churchers, and bros. Multigenerational families, gaggles of girls, hungover yuppies, and Columbia kids. All doing that New York brunch thing on a lovely late-summer day.

WHEN TO GO	Go on a Sunday around noon, *especially* a football Sunday, especially when the weather is fine, the big French doors are wide open, and the beer garden in front is full of people and life. It's a magnificent party inside and out. Inside, you'll have the football-watching crowd, all backslapping their hellos and yelling at the various games on the TVs around the room. Outside, it's all about brunch, and it seems like everyone in town's converging on this corner in Harlem to have a feast, watch their games, and just love life. Bonus: They have live music outside on Saturday and Sunday afternoons. *Happy hour: Monday to Friday, 4 to 7 p.m. $5 select beers, wines, and well drinks, and $7 red sangria.*
WHERE TO SIT	If you're inside, go for the booth area to the far left, up on the fancy little mezzanine. "It's a bit set apart and feels 'VIP,'" says Talley. Plus, raised up there a little, you can see the whole room and, on a football Sunday, every TV in the joint.
WHAT TO DRINK	Out there on the patio, on a bright, sunny day, get something quenching, like Harlem Tavern's Cîroc Celebration, a bubbly cocktail served in a flute glass. Another good bet is punch, served in big old sixteen-ounce Mason jars. Talley recommends either overproof rum or Hennessy punch. They're both popular, and pack quite a *you-know-what*. If you're a fan of slushies, get one of the eight slushy frozen drinks on the menu, including margaritas, daiquiris, Banana Coladas, and Blue Hawaiians.

HARLEM TAVERN

Harlem Tavern Cîroc Celebration

1½ ounces Cîroc Red Berry vodka
1 ounce cranberry juice
½ ounce St-Germain elderflower
    liqueur
Champagne

Combine the vodka, juice, and liqueur in a cocktail shaker with ice. Shake well and strain into a Champagne flute. Top with bubbly and garnish with a cherry.

Subway: The A, B, and C trains stop at Cathedral Parkway (110th Street), six blocks south of Harlem Tavern, and the 2 and 3 trains stop at 116th Street, two blocks east.

The structure at 2153 Frederick Douglass Boulevard used to be an auto body shop, and before that a gas station. Harlem locals Sheri Wilson and her husband, Stephen Daly, walked by that long-dormant neighborhood eyesore several times a day, and a vision took shape. Talley says, "Being partners in several other bars in the city, they were looking to start something of their own, and Harlem Tavern proved to be that place."

HARLEM TAVERN THROWS a PRETTY GOOD ST. PADDY'S DAY BASH, EVEN SHOWCASING A BAND FROM IRELAND A COUPLE YEARS BACK, COMPLETE with a DANCER WHO GOT UP on the TABLE AND PRANCED AWAY. YEAH, YOU'RE THINKING: ST. PADDY'S? IRISH MUSIC? HARLEM?? RIGHT. I GET IT. BUT IT MAKES SENSE. BEFORE HARLEM WAS THE CENTER of NEW YORK'S BLACK CULTURE, IT WAS HOME TO A SIGNIFICANT NUMBER of IRISH, ESPECIALLY in EAST HARLEM.

HARRY'S CAFÉ

1 Hanover Square (between Pearl and Stone Streets)   FINANCIAL DISTRICT, MANHATTAN
harrysnyc.com   ·   *212-785-9200*

HARRY'S IS A CLASSIC DOWNTOWN NEW YORK STEAKHOUSE, opened by Greek immigrant and host supreme Harry Poulakakos in 1972, and now owned by his son, Peter Poulakakos, and his partners. It sprawls throughout the garden level of India House, a private club founded in 1914 by a group of businessmen headed by U.S. Steel's James A. Farrell. The café side of Harry's is the Wall Street bar you'd picture in your head—all wood and leather, brass and glass—even if you've never set foot in New York. It feels strong and secure and confident.

After work, the bar at Harry's is a scene, with a lot of well-dressed financial types (mid-thirties to late sixties) casually enjoying rich after-work snacks like lobster-stuffed mushrooms, steak tartare on toast, and vast platters of shrimp and oysters on cracked ice, all paired with potent drinks served in no-bullshit, straight-walled martini glasses and some very fine wines from Poulakakos's extensive personal cellar.

Now, you could be thinking, *Oh, I see. A* money-guy *bar. Whoop-dee-doo. Too expensive. Not my bag,* etc. And I get that, but I like Harry's. It's elegant, comfortable, gleaming, and gracious, so just take a moment, Swifty, and reconsider your prejudices.

After work—especially on Tuesdays, Wednesdays, and Thursdays—it's a fine place to be. Lively, full of voices and people and the smells of steak and seafood being whipped up by the kitchen for both the restaurant and the bar (they share the same menu), Harry's draws a mature, well-heeled crowd. Noise level is low to medium, mostly conversational, and the soundtrack is a smooth mix of soul, pop, R & B, and jazz from the sixties, seventies, and eighties.

Walking into Harry's for the first time is thrilling. You go down a few steps and leave busy old Hanover Square behind. Push through the rich, polished doors and you feel like you're in a secret place, a rarefied hideout apart from the rest of the world. It feels exclusive (in that grand old 1850s-club-building way), and so do you.

But it's approachable and welcoming nonetheless. The hostess greets you warmly, immediately putting you at ease. Harry himself may be there to say hello, as he still comes in nearly every day of the week. Go to your right and take a seat at the long, glowing mahogany bar. The bartenders, clad in black and white, sleek and professional, give you plenty of time to look at the menu and figure out what you want.

It feels good at Harry's. Special and smooth and strong and luxurious, like a new Cadillac. You're on Wall Street now, baby, the Yankee Stadium of finance. The Show. The baddest, most storied locale in the big league of money. Soak it in. Make like the regulars, indulge a little, and leave feeling like a million bucks.

THE CLIMACTIC MURDER-CONFESSION SCENE *of*
BRET EASTON ELLIS'S 1991 NOVEL, *AMERICAN PSYCHO*,
TAKES PLACE IN HARRY'S *of the* EIGHTIES,
AT THE UNOFFICIAL AFTER-WORK HEADQUARTERS
of WALL STREET'S WILD EIGHTIES BULL RUN.

Tuesday to Thursday, after Wall Street's four p.m. closing bell till about seven.

WHERE **TO** SIT

Dead center at the long bar, facing the windows of post-work commuter frenzy as everyone scurries to trains, ferries, and cars while you casually sip a drink, munch shrimp cocktail, and, watching the folly outside, chuckle drily to yourself.

WHAT **TO** DRINK

Get the classic *New Yorker*–cartoon Wall Street beverage of choice: a martini. An ice-cold, amply garnished Harry's martini. Give that first one a little time to settle, then order an old-fashioned, another traditional dietary staple for businessmen.

HOUSE RECIPE

Harry's Martini

2½ ounces Hendrick's gin
1 ounce Dolin dry vermouth

Stir together the gin and vermouth in a mixing glass full of ice. Lots of ice. You're going for maximum cold and aggressive dilution. Strain into a martini glass and garnish with three big green pitted Cerignola olives on a wooden spike large enough to kill Dracula.

HOW **TO** GET THERE

Subway: The 2 and 3 trains stop at Wall Street, the J and Z trains stop at Broad Street, and the 4 and 5 trains stop at Bowling Green, all within a five-minute walk of Harry's.

WHAT ELSE?

My favorite artifact at Harry's is the signed print of a LeRoy Neiman painting from 1985 showing a roaring crowd at Harry's bar in the artist's unmistakably brash, slashing style. It's a fantastic time capsule of the era, complete with landline phones and boxy monitors above the bar displaying the latest financial stats. The crowd is of the time, too, featuring several famous faces: Felix Rohatyn, the investment banker, Harry Poulakakos, the owner, and Mayor Ed Koch. Neiman had many of the bar's regulars pose for his work, paying them with signed prints of their own. Unfortunately for some, their *bodies* made it into the final art, but not their *heads*. For cases like Koch and Rohatyn, Neiman put their famous faces on top of the models' bodies.

The Post-Work Happy Hour

Some of my best memories of former jobs have nothing whatsoever to do with my time at the office. *Are you kidding me?* They're about going out *after* work with my co-workers. The social connections, the good times, the ridiculous moments. If you can find a group of co-workers who are willing to meet for a tipple after work, you've got something special. Cultivate that scene. *Connecting with other people*—it's what we're here to do, and the old post-work happy hour is key to that.

Years back, I worked a job where the staff had to be a little buttoned-down during the day, but a cadre of instigators—let's call them Dave and Jon and Bob—started a beautiful daily ritual.

Around four in the afternoon, those guys would wrap up their day, hustle to the elevator, tap their wristwatches at me, and mime a large gulp from an invisible pint glass. They'd disappear into the elevator and skedaddle down the street to a pub two blocks from the office. I usually had to work a little later than they did, but that feeling of "something going on" was exciting, and I'd get a happy little charge after I'd wrapped up for the day and headed down to join them.

When I'd get to the bar, they'd be deep into their first or second beer (Labatt Blue, just $1.75 a pint from four to seven), sitting at their usual table by the front window. When I walked in, they'd raise their glasses and let out a joyous, welcoming "HeeeeeEEEEEYYYYY!!"

I miss that sound, that joyful noise, and it buoys my heart now, just writing about it.

It meant, "You're here! Finally! And we're damn glad to see you." And who wouldn't love to hear that after a hard day's work? It's like when Norm walked into Cheers. It's like on *Seinfeld* when the fourth one walked into the diner. It's that feeling of coming home to people who love you. Who doesn't like *that*?

Then the ritual commences: the first beer, the chitchat, the shop talk. The second beer, the wisecracking, the silliness. The freak flags start going up. Maybe someone, let's call him Dave, orders another round for the whole table, usually four to six people from a pool of seven or eight regular attendees, and one happy hour becomes two hours or, on occasion, three.

We'd drink and talk and bitch about work, deconstructing our days and getting to know each other. It made our lives better, it made work better, and friendships grew out of that ritual. You can't bond like that at work, but if you do at ye olde post-work happy hour, you're sure to be a happier employee, surrounded by friends at work, not just co-workers.

Cultivate the post-work happy hour, I say! Find a joint near your workplace and get the ball rolling with a couple others. Just have one drink and see how that goes. Stick with it! Try to go at least once or twice every week, and see who else joins in. I promise you that if your post-work happy hour becomes a regular thing, you'll have a better workplace, enjoy the workday more, and make some good friends.

HI-LIFE BAR AND GRILL

477 Amsterdam Avenue (at West Eighty-third Street)   UPPER WEST SIDE, MANHATTAN
hi-life.com   ·   *212-787-7199*

YOU KNOW YOU'RE IN FOR SOMETHING SPECIAL when you approach a bar with neon sprawling across the entire length of its facade. That intense glow draws your eye and lures you in. Duck into the Hi-Life Bar and Grill and you'll enter another era. It's set up like a classic corner tavern, circa 1945: a solid wooden bar to your right, booths and banquettes to your left, the walls loaded with cheesecakey pinups, photos of midcentury boxers, and a black velvet portrait of Frank Sinatra. It's a riot of prime Americana from the Greatest Generation, the fruition of owner Earl Geer's passion.

"My vision was 'working-class elegance,'" says Geer, who opened Hi-Life in 1991. "I wanted the place to have that sort of thirties 'old man' vibe. In my mind's eye, the owner would've had his own fish tank in here, then he'd've caught a marlin in Key West, had it mounted, and shoved it down everyone's throat." (Said marlin is above the breezeway as you walk in, north of the fish tank and between two potted palms.) He took inspiration from the once ubiquitous "steaks and chops" taverns that dotted New York from the thirties to the sixties but that were—as tastes changed—sold, remodeled, or torn down to make way for shiny condos, nail salons, juice bars, or yet another convenient branch of your favorite megabank.

"I loved the architecture and feeling of those places," says Geer. "I wanted to bring back something that was fading from New York City." He created the Hi-Life out of a space that had been a Thai restaurant in the eighties (and before that a gay bar, and before that a topless joint, and before even *that* a classic bar and grill called the Luxor), then tricked it out in the style of long-gone classics like McHale's Bar in Hell's Kitchen and Harlem's Lenox Lounge. "They tore the shit out of that place," he says sadly, looking at a black-and-white photo of the Lenox hanging on the wall.

Okay, no tears. Thanks to Geer, we have a damn fine re-creation of an old-time New York bar and grill in the heart of the Upper West Side, complete with button-tufted wall panels, staffers "hired for eccentricity," and a raw bar with fresh clams and oysters *and* expertly prepared sushi. Didn't see that coming, did you? Geer explains: "I realized that a raw bar was often a complement to steaks and chops. Sushi was a thing in the late eighties/early nineties, so I said, 'Let's have our own raw bar run by a Japanese sushi chef with not only sushi, but also clams and oysters shucked to order.'" The whole thing works.

Go for happy hour, slide into the dinner rush, soak up that old New York flavor (along with a big ol' martini), and be grateful that someone's keeping the steaks-and-chops-bar-and-grill tradition alive. With sushi.

It's set up like a classic corner tavern, circa 1945:
a solid wooden bar to your right, booths AND *banquettes to your left,*
the walls loaded with cheesecakey pinups, photos OF
midcentury boxers, AND *a black velvet portrait* OF *Frank Sinatra.*

HI-LIFE BAR AND GRILL

WHEN TO GO

Friday around five or six, when you can still get a seat and enjoy a civilized happy hour during the lull before the storm. By ten "the roof is comin' off the place," as Geer puts it, which can be a hell of a good time, too.

Happy hour: Daily, 4 to 7 p.m. $6 select specialty cocktails, well drinks, house wine, and domestic draft pints. $6 hors d'oeuvres and small plates, too, like the sliders/sushi combo, oysters, clams, nachos, and "Chinatown ribs."

WHERE TO SIT

Table one, the horseshoe-shaped booth to the left of the door as you walk in. It's a cozy spot for you and your friends, with a great view of the room—and a little snug harbor when things get hoppin', too.

WHAT TO DRINK

You're in a deco-inspired tavern represented by a martini glass on the neon sign out front. Don't screw around, bub. Get a real drink, like a martini or a Gibson, made big and served up in a cocktail glass, with a little extra in a "sidecar" carafe on ice. (Bonus: The generous serving of six "drunken" olives or cocktail onions that come with your drink, soaked for days—sometimes *weeks*—in vodka or gin.) Then, when you're good and warmed up, get something wacky like the White Cosmo, a refreshing, powerful concoction, also served with the sidecar kicker.

HOUSE RECIPE

White Cosmo

4 ounces Absolut Citron
2 ounces white cranberry juice
Splash of St-Germain elderflower
  liqueur

Combine all the ingredients in a cocktail shaker with ice. Shake vigorously, and I mean really beat the hell out of it. Strain into a large, chilled martini glass and serve with a lemon twist. Save the remainder to refresh your drink.

HOW TO GET THERE

Subway: The 1 train stops at 86th Street, or take the B or C to the 81st–Museum of Natural History stop, both four blocks from Hi-Life.

Geer, an aficionado of old neon, went to the source to get his sign for Hi-Life: Artkraft Strauss on West Fifty-seventh Street, the company behind most of the eye-popping "spectaculars" of Times Square and, in fact, much of the neon signage throughout New York City and around the world over the past century. Geer approached them with his vision, and they in turn gave him several archival photos of signs they'd created over the years. One was for Jordan's, a midcentury New York corner bar. Upon closer inspection, Geer recognized the corner: Eighty-third and Amsterdam, right across the street from today's Hi-Life, then known as the Luxor.

Lushy laughs: Every Hi-Life menu includes an old cartoon featuring their signature drink, the martini. In my favorite (by Henry Martin), a sixtyish businessman is sitting at a bar. "It was a very bleak period in my life, Louie," he says to the bartender. "Martinis didn't help. Religion didn't help. Psychiatry didn't help. Transcendental meditation didn't help. Yoga didn't help. But Martinis helped a little."

KEEP YOUR EYES PEELED AND YOU MAY CATCH A GLIMPSE of the HI-LIFE MOBILE, GEER'S 1936 LINCOLN ZEPHYR, TOPPED with a DOUBLE-SIDED VERSION of the HI-LIFE'S GLOWING SIGN, NEON MARTINI GLASS AND ALL. KIND OF HARD TO MISS, EVEN IN NEW YORK.

J.G. MELON

1291 Third Avenue (at East Seventy-fourth Street)   UPPER EAST SIDE, MANHATTAN
jgmelonnyc.com · *212-744-0585*

YOU WALK INTO J.G. MELON WHEN IT'S HOPPIN', and, Jack, it is *hoppin'*. Cacophonous pandemonium. A madhouse. And yet you commit yourself, because it feels like *the* place to be. You don't *go* there when it's busy if you don't want to *be* there when it's busy, and it's busy a lot. That's half the fun, being *where it's at*.

The front room is narrow and loud and overflowing with stimuli: music coming at you from the old jukebox, the flagrantly enticing aroma of sizzling beef, melon-centric art all over the walls (dozens and dozens of pieces, from the red tin ceiling on down), and people, people, people. The bar juts in deep from the left, making the joint feel that much more crowded. The hungry are everywhere, waiting, scooching in, scooching out, getting seated, eating, drinking, yakking, cackling. Scads of humans: Upper East Siders, tourists, bros, kooks, geeks, first-timers, long-timers, old-timers. Moms, dads, kids, DINKs, goofballs, grumps, grouches, weenies, you, me. (If you think hell is other people, stay home, Jean-Paul.) They're all there at Melon's RIGHT WHEN YOU ARE, and they want The Burger, but more on that later.

First, the origin story. How do you create an instant classic in New York's tough restaurant market? Location, timing, and an irresistible hook. Melon's founders, the late Jack O'Neill and George Mourges, opened it in 1972 at Seventy-fourth Street and Third Avenue, near their employer at the time, a restaurant on the wane. "They saw it was going downhill," says Shaun Young, longtime J.G. Melon general manager and partner, now a co-owner of Melon's downtown satellite. "They put their money together to open a new place so they'd have a job." They set up in what had been the Central Bar, an old corner tavern with thirties character and charm, right there in the heart of the Upper East Side, one of New York's steadiest, most affluent neighborhoods, even during the fiscally choppy seventies.

The partners tricked the place out in a now iconic deep green, the color of a summer watermelon, from the exterior down to the checked tablecloths. They hung four antique prints of watermelons on the wall, which got the melon ball rolling. (And rolling. And *rolling*.) And the name? *J* for Jack, *G* for George, and *Melon* for the art.

The Burger (details to follow; hold your horses) started getting attention, especially when nearby fancy-pants restaurant Mortimer's closed for its annual two-week summer break, sending some of their well-heeled patrons flocking to Melon's. The Burger knocked them out, and they told everyone. Pretty soon "society people" (as Young calls them) started showing up: the rich, the connected, the powerful.

Young says, "These people weren't used to waiting," but J.G. Melon was a hit and everyone had to be patient. "Grace Kelly came in with a friend once in the seventies," he recalls. "We had a thirty-minute wait, so she just hopped up onto the old jukebox with a Heineken, sat, and waited."

Celebrities started showing up regularly: Jackie O, her kids John and Caroline, Walter Cronkite, Matt Lauer. Mayors, senators, governors, congressmen, and the occasional president. Andre Agassi, Brooke Shields, Jerry Seinfeld. "We never called Page Six," Young says, referring to the *New York Post's* tattletale gossip section. "That's why they came." And, of course, for The Burger.

Okay, The Burger: Jack O'Neill, who possessed "an outstanding palate," as Young puts it, insisted on creating an outstanding hamburger. He sat down with one of New York's best butchers, Sammy Solasz of Master Purveyors meat market, and came up with the signature blend still used today: Black Angus chuck "and other cuts I can't tell ya," according to Young. O'Neill would test a raw bite of every daily delivery, once sending back four hundred pounds that didn't meet his standards. He passed that duty on to Young, who still does it today, tasting for flavor before cooking and after, and, importantly, gauging for an ideal 17 to 18 percent fat content. He nails it. Has to. That burger is the key to the whole operation, the loosely packed, perfectly griddle-seared wonder that holds the J.G. Melon universe together.

SEE THE BRASS PLAQUES WITH NAMES on the WALL ABOVE THE BAR? "A GUY CAME IN EVERY DAY for THREE WEEKS, STUDIED THOSE PLAQUES, and FINALLY SAID, 'WHAT DO I HAVE TO DO TO GET MY NAME UP THERE?'" YOUNG TOLD HIM, "DIE." THOSE PLAQUES ARE TRIBUTES to LOYAL CUSTOMERS (AND THE FOUNDERS, JACK AND GEORGE) WHO'VE PASSED ON.

WHEN TO GO

Saturday or Sunday afternoon, or any weekday after 6:30 p.m.

Happy hour: Monday to Friday, 3 to 7 p.m. Food specials plus $1 off well drinks, house wines, and most beers.

WHERE TO SIT

I prefer any seat I can get at the bar. Better service during the rush, and it's almost always the rush at Melon's.

Open with a Bloody Bull. It's like a Bloody Mary made with a combo of tomato juice and beef consommé. It's not spicy, and involves no horseradish or hot sauce. Instead, it's smooth and rich, a good warm-up for your meal to come. Next drink: have a draft beer in one of those heavy, chilled glass mugs to go with your burger.

J.G. Melon Bloody Bull

Nothing is measured; the bartender eyeballs the proportions. "We pour a pretty heavy drink," says Young.

2-plus ounces well vodka
About 2 ounces Campbell's
*   beef broth*
About 2 ounces Sacramento-brand
*   tomato juice*
About ¾ ounce fresh lemon juice
4 or 5 "strong" dashes of
*   Worcestershire sauce*

Combine all the ingredients in a tall glass full of ice, then mix by pouring it all into another tall glass and back again. Garnish with a lime wedge.

Subway: The 6 train stops at 77th Street, four blocks away.

True story: During a dinner rush in 1975, Young got a call. "Guy's on the phone and says, 'The president wants to eat at Melon's and will be there in five minutes.' I say, 'Look, we're full. We got a twenty- to thirty-minute wait.' He says, *'The president will be there in five minutes.'* I say, 'Okay, then.' We set up a table and the president—Ford it was—shows up with his wife, has dinner—very nice couple—and when they're leaving, Mrs. Ford has to use the ladies' room. President Ford is waiting, and we talk for a few minutes. They leave and the guys ask me, 'What were you talking about with the president for ten minutes?' I say, 'Burgers.' The president wanted to talk about burgers."

If the uptown J.G. Melon is too packed or too far away, you can enjoy a damn good (and roomier) version at MacDougal and Bleeker Streets in the heart of the West Village. It's got a similar decor: tin ceiling the red of a ripe melon's interior, melon-y artwork on the walls, and the iconic green-checked tablecloths. The Burger is the same Master Purveyors blend, ground fresh daily, then cooked and served the tried-and-true way.

JIMMY'S CORNER

140 West Forty-fourth Street (between Sixth Avenue and Broadway)   TIMES SQUARE, MANHATTAN
212-221-9510

SQUEEZE INTO JIMMY'S CORNER AT THE END OF A WORKDAY and roll with it. Trust me. It's going to be crowded. You got a problem with that? It's crowded for a reason: people love it. It's a dive, sure, and I mean that in the best way. It's a narrow old room, but with luck you won't have to suck in your gut too long, as you might get a spot at the long bar to your left. If not, well, keep suckin' and move to the back of the bus. Keep moving, keep moving. There's a whole 'nother room in there. Back, back, back, past the bar, past the hundreds of photos of boxing legends. Past the fabled old CD jukebox, up the stairs, and into the back room, also skinny and tight, but blessed with a few small tables and some chairs. Got a seat yet? No? Well, just hold your beer close, feed the jukebox, and wait. The crowd'll thin out in a little bit.

Enjoy it. You're in a special place. All these people wouldn't be here if it weren't, amiright? Jimmy's is unlike any other venue within spittin' distance of Times Square. It's been a bar forever. In fact, Jimmy Lee Glenn himself met his late wife, Swannie—Swietlana Garbarski, from Poland—back in the sixties when she was bartending here and the joint was called Club 140, for the address. They fell in love, got married, and picked up the lease when 140 closed. (Same landlords to this day; they love Jimmy's, which is why it's still here.) Jimmy also ran a boxing gym on Forty-second Street back in the day, then went into the bar business, and he and Swannie had a kid, Adam, who they raised a few blocks west.

Adam grew up like any New York City kid of the eighties—watching hustlers and junkies and pick-pockets from his window, running around Times Square, having fun. His dad was known as the Mayor of Forty-fourth Street, and Adam was more or less a free-range city kid. No one messed with him and everyone knew who he was: Jimmy and Swannie's son. He was smart, and so was his dad, who wouldn't let him go into boxing. Instead, Adam graduated from Harvard Law, took a job in mergers and acquisitions, and did all right for himself. After his mom died, he quit his money job and started helping his dad at the bar. And he loves it.

"Jimmy's is my home as much as the house I grew up in," he says. "I love everything about it. I love that my parents met here and they built it into an institution together. I love the fact that I learned so much here, from what it was to work hard to how to deal with people. As a bar, I love the diversity and how down-to-earth it is. You can have a CEO sitting next to a homeless person, and they're treated the same way and get to have the same experience." He adds, "If you're easygoing and enjoy a good cheap drink in a fun, laid-back bar, then you'll be happy at Jimmy's."

Once you find a spot to settle in, you will be happy indeed. The place is a rough sort of joyous, a regular dog's breakfast of things and color and people. Neon glows in the window. Christmas lights that never come down glimmer above the wall behind the bar. Look up and see several U.S. flags, dollar bills tacked up here and there, a set of Ringside-brand gloves, and old posters and photos of boxers all over the place. Roberto Durán, Leon Spinks, Oscar De La Hoya, Sugar Ray Leonard, Tommy "Hit-man" Hearns, Marvelous Marvin Hagler, and, of course, the Greatest—Muhammad Ali. There he is, all smiling and genial with Jimmy. There he is again, giving Jimmy the old "pop on the chin" pose with his mighty right.

You might not see Jimmy around the bar in the flesh as much these days, with Adam and the rest of the staff now more or less running the show, but he's there in a hundred pictures, posing with friends, fans, and fighters. He's up on the walls, he's behind the bar. And look down: he's *on* the bar, too, in a collage of photos like layers of peeling wallpaper in the living room of an old New York brownstone—pictures going back to 1971, if you look carefully. That's Jimmy's work, that collage, like this bar is. Layers and layers of people and memories and good times, soaked in whiskey and beer and tons of love.

"We're a place that's comfortable being what we are," says Adam. "And we never try to pretend to be something else, and I think that's rare." Hear, hear! [A toast to Jimmy: *clink*.] Another Bud Light, please.

WHY'S THE JUKEBOX SO LEGENDARILY GOOD? BECAUSE JIMMY CURATES IT, THAT'S WHY. IT'S ONLY FULL of STUFF HE HAS PERSONALLY OKAYED OVER THE DECADES, SO YOU'VE GOT A COLLECTION OF MUSIC IN THAT MACHINE THAT A HUMAN *with* HEART AND TASTE HAS PERSONALLY VOUCHED FOR. "NOTHING GETS IN THERE UNLESS HE APPROVES OF IT," ACCORDING *to* ADAM GLENN.

WHEN TO GO	Get the full experience: Go to Jimmy's Corner at five on a weekday afternoon and plan to hang around a bit. The place fills up in a big way right after work, and it gets crowded, "a turn-off to some people," Adam admits, "because the place is so small." Suits, blue collars, creatives. Young, old, rich, poor, everyone goes to Jimmy's. Then, around seven, the crowd starts to thin out, the place quiets down a little, and you will get a seat and move on to the talking and jukebox-feeding portion of your evening.
WHERE TO SIT	"Definitely the end of the bar to your left as you walk in," says Adam. "You can see everything and no one bumps into you."
WHAT TO DRINK	Start with a bottle of Bud and a shot of Jameson. Settle in, and follow that up with . . . another beer. "Keep it simple when you're here," Adam advises. There are four brews on tap and several in bottles, all cheap. Enjoy.
HOW TO GET THERE	Subway: The 1, 2, 3, 7, N, Q, R, and W trains all stop just three blocks away at Times Square–42nd Street. The B, D, F, and M trains stop four blocks away at 42nd Street–Bryant Park.
WHAT ELSE?	Remember that awful/great/awful scene in *Raging Bull* where Robert De Niro as Jake LaMotta does his post-boxing career "comedy" patter while emceeing at some seedy little club? He's all puffy and vulgar and sleazy and crude, getting heckled by the disinterested, half-drunk barflies, and he just keeps swearing at them and doing his crappy jokes, and it goes on and on and *on*? (God, it hurts to even *think* about it.) That scene was filmed at Jimmy's, with De Niro standing on the top step that leads to the back room, to the right of the jukebox.
	For a place that's as crowded and boozy as Jimmy's is, it's pretty rare to hear a cross conversation. I mean, I've heard people discussing *cannibalism* there, *with* the bartender no less, but it was *civilized*, you know what I mean? It might be owned by a retired boxer, but this isn't a place for fights. And there's one thing you're *not* going to hear discussed at Jimmy's—thank God—and that's politics. See the sign up there behind the bar? It's just a crummy piece of eight and a half by eleven dog-eared copier paper, but its message is powerful: LET'S NOT DISCUSS POLITICS HERE. 'Nuff said.

JOYCE'S TAVERN

3823 Richmond Avenue (between Wilson Avenue and Coryn Court)   ELTINGVILLE, STATEN ISLAND
joycestavern.com   ·   *718-948-0220*

WE'RE STANDING AT THE BAR AT JOYCE'S TAVERN—me, Colleen, our friends Juan and Tony, and Tony's mom, Virginia, who trekked over from her house, where Tony grew up, just a few blocks away. After a while the front door opens up, and an old man with a walker pushes in, making his way slowly toward the back. Before he gets to where he's going, a guy slides off his bar stool and moves down a couple, and the bartender, a big guy with a Mount Rushmore chin, draws a beer and sets it in front of the vacated seat. The old guy slides onto the stool, nods a thanks to the bartender, and all is well.

"Yeah, that was Mr. Toomey," owner Joe O'Toole, Sr. tells me. "He's a retired FDNY lieutenant. Bud drinker. He calls before he shows up and asks if anyone's in front. That means 'move your damn car,' so he can park there and be close to the front door."

That's the beauty of the old neighborhood tavern. It belongs to The People. Technically, Joyce's now belongs to the O'Toole family, who bought it after founder Robert Joyce (always referred to as Mr. Joyce) passed away in 2015. But the *tradition*, that belongs to everyone. To the regulars, to the Eltingville neighborhood, to Staten Island. The sign out front says it all: THE O'TOOLE FAMILY/JOYCE'S TAVERN/ KEEPING THE TRADITION ALIVE.

It's a family place, run by a clan who all pitch in to make it work, and that's getting scarcer by the year in this city, where rising rents often push out small family-owned businesses in favor of corporate operations, or businesses with deep-pocketed partners. But a real, family-run business? That's become rare.

Before Mr. Joyce died, he gave the O'Tooles his blessing to buy the tavern. Joe Sr. even delivered Mr. Joyce's eulogy, and later that year the O'Tooles added their family name to the sign. The sons of Joe and his wife, Claire, help out, too, and Mom and Dad recently gifted Joe Jr. and Ken shares in the business, "for all they have done to keep the tradition alive."

Joyce's is an old-fashioned place, clean and orderly, with a crocheted 1776 U.S. flag on the wall, made by Mrs. Joyce herself in 1976 for the Bicentennial; a back room nicknamed "Tammany Hall" used for business and pleasure by local clubs, cops, and firemen; and a jukebox that can be overridden by the bartender if anything too weird gets played. (You'll get a refund if you ask.) It's where people go for wakes, for receptions, for reunions. Joe Sr. says, "It's the best place in the world to bring a date. It's got a great reputation. When people come back to the neighborhood, they come to Joyce's."

JOYCE'S IS SO IRISH THAT IN ADDITION *to the* USUAL ST. PATRICK'S DAY PARTY, THEY ALSO HOST A "HALFWAY *to* ST. PATRICK'S DAY" BASH EVERY SEPTEMBER.

WHEN TO GO

Stop in at 4:30 or 5 p.m. on a weekday and see the place during the post-work rush. O'Toole says, "That's when all the people getting off the train come in, and the retirees after their chores for the day are done." There's always live entertainment at Joyce's on Thursday, Friday, and Saturday nights, usually bands playing pop from the fifties, sixties, and seventies, or traditional Irish music.

WHERE TO SIT

At the back half of the bar, near the door leading out to the deck. There, you're near the taps and within a quick strike of the jukebox, with the fireplace at your back, a blessing in the winter. But if Mr. Toomey comes in and wants his seat, move on down.

WHAT TO DRINK

A Guinness, boyo! What else? Follow that up with a little Jameson Irish whiskey. Joyce's carries six or seven varieties of it.

HOW TO GET THERE

The Staten Island Railway stops half a block away, at the Eltingville station. To get to Staten Island, take the free ferry from the Whitehall Terminal in Manhattan. Of course, driving is a fine option, too, via the Verrazano-Narrows Bridge from Brooklyn.

WHAT ELSE?

Mr. Joyce was a cat lover, and the cat he loved most was Coco, a rare male calico. A "money cat" that people used to pet for good luck. There's a picture of Mr. Joyce and Coco over the fireplace in the main room. Every year Mr. Joyce threw a birthday party for Coco, with an open bar and a spread of food for twenty-five dollars. Regulars were sort of required to be there (or risk Mr. Joyce's ire), and the proceeds went to local animal shelters. When Coco was getting old and on his way out, someone gave Mr. Joyce another cat, Katie, who you might still see hanging around the fine back deck behind the tavern. "They knew Mr. Joyce wouldn't be good without a cat," Joe Sr. told me.

Day Drinking vs. Night Drinking

I'm a fan of good old wholesome day drinking. Have been since college, when I waded, awkwardly, into those waters, never having done much drinking in high school, or elementary school or preschool, for that matter.

Anyway, this book is about having some nice, social time while enjoying a drink, not about getting wrecked. This means judicious use of the drug known as alcohol. If there's any doubt in your mind why day drinking beats the after-hours version, please see the points below.

DAY DRINKING	NIGHT DRINKING
Plenty of time ahead of you. No rush. Pacing is leisurely and relaxed.	The clock is ticking. Last call looms. Bad decisions are made concerning frequency of ordering. Someone shows up with two rounds of shots called Dirty Girl Scouts.
Slower pacing yields moderation, known since antiquity as the key to happiness.	Abject drunkenness is a distinct possibility and must be guarded against. This hovers over true carefree fun like the Sword of Damocles.
Vitamin D! ("Thanks, Mr. Sun!")	Vitamin Regret.
Laughs, wit, *bon mots*, lighthearted tomfoolery, and the occasional innocent shenanigan.	Between midnight and four in the morning, poor cognition leads to all manner of horrors, bad judgment—and even worse decisions—among them.
One or two full meals (plus snacks) still lie ahead of you, delivering you much-needed ballast, nutrition, and the rejuvenating properties of salt, fat, and starch.	Your best meals are behind you and may indeed come back to haunt you in spectacular fashion.
Plenty of time to sober up and get a good night's sleep.	Kiss your eight-solid-hours good-bye. Horrible, fitful sleep, if any, awaits.
Tomorrow holds the promise of glory.	Tomorrow promises to be gory.

THE KEEP

205 Cypress Avenue (between Starr Street and Willoughby Avenue)   RIDGEWOOD, QUEENS
718-381-0400

HANGING OUT AT THE KEEP IS LIKE SPENDING TIME in another dimension. It's *in* our world, but not quite *of* our world. Your eyes adjust to the soft lights of the large room, and you begin to notice what you smell: hundreds of old things, treasures and curiosities, on the walls, on shelves, on the floors. Things to look at, things to touch, things to sit on. It's like a fantastic antique shop with a full bar run by an Edward Gorey character. Or maybe a long-forgotten alternate set for the old *Addams Family* TV show. The place has sexy–funky–purple–velvet–flocked velour style.

Sit down, look around, and take it all in: faded red Radio Flyer "hot rods" that you wish you had had when you were a kid, Gothic-looking birdcages, creaky old perambulators, vaguely funereal dried flowers, spooky dolls, Edison phonographic cylinders in canisters with Thomas himself smiling from the labels. A fancy spoon collection hanging in a dark wooden display rack, a mysterious plaque that reads "1942," a model ship surrounded by legal tender, a sign advertising DRUGS AND SUNDRIES, a busted bust whose face belies *the pain, oh, the pain.* . . . A miniature Pee-wee Herman sitting casually next to a stuffed fox twice his size, a human skull, a desiccated alligator head, a tiny fat man in a black suit trapped forever beneath a bell jar. A copper lion's head frozen in a never-ending growl, a perplexed-looking stuffed ferret (I think), a couple mysterious dark globes, several lanterns, a fleet of rusty tricycles, and a little reproduction of contender Luis Firpo knocking the champ Jack Dempsey clean out of the ring, as painted by George Wesley Bellows in 1924.

And that's just *some* of the stuff above and around the bar *alone*. Multiply that by thirty or forty or maybe one hundred and you'll get an idea of the abundance at the Keep, none of it junk. It's all thoughtfully chosen and tastefully weird.

Stephanie Jankowitz-Castillo and her husband, Diego Castillo, opened the Keep in 2014 after living in Ridgewood for ten years. With help from friends, they decorated the vast space—once a restaurant with a notorious past—floor to ceiling with treasures Stephanie had collected and kept at home over the previous thirty years. Scouting thrift shops, antique stores, and resale venues in "every country and city [she] ever visited," Stephanie collected a massive trove of "objects that seemed to say 'take me with you!'" These are objects with positive energy, and lots of it, which is why she chose them in the first place. The Keep is loaded with good stuff with good vibes.

The drink menu is a grimoiric list of "Potions & Elixirs," with the "Medicinal Magick & Benefits" of herbal ingredients like lavender, juniper, and rosemary explained on the back. Diego crafted the

It's like a fantastic antique shop *with a* full bar run by an Edward Gorey character.
Or maybe a long-forgotten alternate set *for the* old *Addams Family* TV show.
The place has sexy—funky—purple—velvet—flocked velour style.

THE KEEP

well-considered drink menu, and, according to Stephanie, he "speaks well wishes and prayers over every mixture as he simmers the fresh ginger and lavender" and other ingredients for the cocktails.

The place is marvelously strange, kind of spiritual, and imbued with intention and love. But that doesn't mean it's not fun. I assure you, it's fun.

We popped by on a demonically hot day in late summer, our curiosity piqued by a whiteboard on the sidewalk in front, the message more like a wordy Victorian carnival poster than the postmodern one-liners most bars sport these days. Once inside and acclimated to our new dimension, we hung out with barkeep Glennie Blackshire, she of the flaxen tresses straight out of *Game of Thrones*.

After we'd feasted on the magickal sights and partaken of the tasty potions, we left to grab a bite down the street and investigate another bar in nearby Bushwick, but we were lured back to the Keep, enchanted. There, we spent the rest of that evening sipping the night away with Glennie and the bar's youngish, tattooed patrons.

WHEN TO GO	Sunday afternoon, or any night when something wonderful is happening, which is generally *every* night. The Keep hosts live nightly DJs like Shakey and Illexxandra, $mall¢hange, DJ Baby K, JoroBoro, Nappy G, Spliffington & TriceCat, and Justin Case, to name a few. Then there are occasional events like the Thrift ON! clothing swap parties, Film Noir nights, Drunk Yoga on Saturday mornings, Séance Sundays, and tarot readings by folks like Darcey Leonard of the Tarot Society. **Bonus:** *On Sundays when the weather's warm and they're grilling out back, enjoy a complimentary hot dog, burger, or sausage with every drink you buy. Just be sure to tip the grill guy. (Karma comes back, man.)*
WHERE TO SIT	I think sitting at the bar is charming. Stephanie suggests the Victorian love seats by the mock fireplace.
WHAT TO DRINK	Start off with the Lavender, a calming yet refreshing cocktail made with fresh ginger and lavender. To go with your Sunday eats from the grill (or any old time), get the shot-and-beer special. Last I did, it was a can of Lionshead beer (echoing the growling-lion pediment above the bar in front of me) and a shot of bourbon.

THE KEEP

Subway: The L train stops at Jefferson Street, just a three-minute walk up Starr Street to the Keep.

True story: Back in the sixties, 205 Cypress Avenue wasn't a cozy, magical bar, but a Greek restaurant called the Cypress Gardens, and it catered to some pretty rough characters. Among them were three associates of the Bonanno crime family: Jimmy D'Angelo, his brother Tommy, and Frankie "500" Telleri. On the night of November 10, 1969, all three were shot dead as they met at the Cypress Gardens, mowed down by twenty-five rounds from a .45-caliber submachine gun wielded by a man in a black raincoat and a dark fedora. As they bled out, the shooter left, never to be positively identified. You can still see bullet holes from that night to your right as you walk into the Keep. "I put antique windows on the wall," says Stephanie, "and we *created* over it, so you can still see the bullet holes. I know that's kind of maca-bre, but I appreciated the history."

Notice the smiling stuffed hyena high on the brick wall to the left of the bar. That is a special little guy. Stephanie explains why: "I love Hanni-bal, our male hyena who—oddly—lived a long life and died of natural causes before he was taxidermied." (At least that's what she was told by the guy who sold it to her.) I, for one, am delighted to believe this story of the happy hyena who peacefully passed away at home, surrounded by loved ones—as opposed to shot up like a Bonanno associate—before he was stuffed, mounted, and displayed at the Keep for patrons' bemusement.

A THOUGHTFUL TOUCH: STEPHANIE EMBEDDED DOZENS of PENNIES, FACE UP, ALL ALONG the BAR'S PERIMETER, "SO EVERYONE WHO SITS THERE CAN GET SOME GOOD LUCK," SHE EXPLAINS.

THE KETTLE BLACK

8622 Third Avenue (at Eighty-seventh Street)   BAY RIDGE, BROOKLYN
kettleblackbar.com   ·   718-680-7862

FIRST TIME WE EVER WENT TO THE KETTLE BLACK, we were deep in Bay Ridge early on a Sunday afternoon and we hadn't eaten yet. From the sidewalk on Third Avenue, we saw tables full of diners through the big floor-to-ceiling windows of the bar, which our friend Pappas, a Bay Ridge local, had recommended to us.

We headed in for brunch and saw a group of eight or ten guys up front at the bar, all watching the Mets, who were in second place just then, five games behind the Nationals, whom they were playing that afternoon. The guys were into it: drinking beer, hollering, and groaning as the Mets played like the Mets.

In the big front room, far to the left, past two brick columns, was the brunch crowd: a couple of families with the kids, a group of twentysomething girls, a table of ladies, and a date or two. The waitress, a local named Jenn, gave us a high-top at a window facing Eighty-seventh, and we proceeded to tie on the feedbag.

Brunch was a damn delight, but what struck me about the place was the different ways people were using it, yet they all seemed at home. The guys at the bar were treating the joint like their man cave, drinking beer, yelling at the TV, and having a good old time. The brunchers were equally content with their omelets, pancakes, Bloodys, coffee, and black skillets full of chow. "We're a perfect sports bar," Jenn explained. "There's not a place where you don't have a good TV view, but people love our brunch, too."

Next time we went, it was late on a Friday night, and the place was apeshit: packed, loud, and rowdy. Mostly locals, twenty-five to forty, blowing off steam after a long, hot workweek. But that's the beauty of a local's local: everyone uses the place how they want, whether that's watching the game, having a chill brunch, eating dinner with the kids (Wing Wednesday is immensely popular at the Kettle Black), or boozing it up with your buddies on weekend nights.

"Yeah, we're a neighborhood bar," says co-owner Chris King. "We get mostly neighborhood families, blue-collar guys, civil servants." The four owners are all Bay Ridge guys: two Wall Streeters and two firefighters, all retired. Three of them are cousins, and the other they've known since high school. Locally owned, locally supported, but not so local that you won't have a good time there if you're a visitor. Use it how you want.

"I like our diversity," King went on. "You know, on Sundays, we get all types in here." *Oh, yeah?* "Yeah, Bills fans, Steelers fans, Eagles fans. Hey, I'm a *Cowboys* fan, if you can believe that! We all get along and break each other's chops. It's great."

THE guys AT THE *bar were treating the joint like their man cave, drinking beer, yelling at the TV, and having a good old time. The brunchers were equally content* WITH *their omelets, pancakes, Bloodys, coffee,* AND *black skillets full of chow.*

Sunday afternoons in the fall. Come for the brunch. Stay for the football.

"Stool one," says King, "the first high-top table in the main barroom. People reserve it two weeks in advance for big games like the Super Bowl. It's the best because you can see the whole room and every TV screen."

They pour a real good Guinness at Kettle Black. Don't want a beer? All right. Go for a Skinny Dip. Yeah. I said it.

Skinny Dip

About a 3-count of Deep Eddy sweet tea vodka (That's about 3 ounces. Generous pours at the KB!)
About a 2-count of water
A splash of lemon simple syrup (2 parts each of water and sugar and 1 part fresh lemon juice, stirred or shaken until the sugar completely dissolves)

Combine all the ingredients in a highball glass filled with ice. Stir. Garnish with a lemon wedge.

Subway: The R train stops at 86th Street, two blocks away.

The Kettle Black's chicken wings are legendary, and the bar was named one of the top five wing joints in America by none other than *Food & Wine* magazine in 2015. "Yeah, we pride ourselves on making great wings, but we had no idea *that'd* happened," King says. "One day our phones start blowin' up!" They've got about a dozen styles to choose from, including original Buffalo City, Luau, Chuckwagon, Ragin' Cajun, and Grandpa Nunzio's, with garlic, butter, and shaved Parmesan. Order twelve wings and you can choose two different kinds; if you're a first-timer, get the traditional Buffalo style and Grandpa Nunzio's. Hey, where else are you gonna find *Grandpa Nunzio's* wings, huh?

KILLMEYER'S OLD BAVARIA INN

4254 Arthur Kill Road (at Sharrotts Road) CHARLESTON, STATEN ISLAND
killmeyers.com · *718-984-1202*

YOU MIGHT THINK WHEN A MODERN-DAY PLACE in New York City—on Staten Island, no less—calls itself "old" and "Bavaria" right there in its name, that it's just a gimmick. Like a tourist bar trying to be all "Old West" by calling itself something like Jebediah P. Leathersmacker's Old-Tyme Cowpoke Saloon. This is not the case with Killmeyer's. It's legitimately German *and* quite old, in operation in one form or another at this location since 1859, according to owner Ken Tirado.

Back in the eighteen hundreds, the neighborhood—and much of Staten Island—was loaded with German immigrants who made good use of the island's fresh spring waters for brewing. The heavy clay soil in the southwest was ideal for manufacturing firebricks, and the area blossomed as a German-American brick factory town called Kreischerville, named for brick baron Balthasar Kreischer. During the anti-German blowback following World War I, the neighborhood's name was changed to the über-English-sounding Charleston.

When Tirado bought the place in 1995, it was a roadhouse bar and music venue called the Century Inn. Tirado decided to honor Staten Island's heritage by bringing the German back to Kreischerville, and Killmeyer's—the business's original name when it was a store, saloon, and hotel run by the family who built it—was reborn. "We figured that since there were no more German restaurants on the island," Tirado says, "a Bavarian beer hall would be unique."

Killmeyer's offers a couple of different ways to enjoy *das gute* life: indoors, with that old-world woody dining room/bar feel, and outdoors, in the beer garden, which operates from May through the end of October. The inside is *wunderbar*, with all the German touches, the moose head, and the gorgeous old mahogany bar, but if you want to experience Killmeyer's in all its glory, visit on a beautiful day and hit the beer garden.

Tirado paid attention to detail when he crafted that beer garden, paving it with rectangular stones, getting the gazebo bar just right, nailing the visuals overall. He spent years doing set design for theater and visual merchandising, after all, and went to Munich to do his homework—and it shows. In the right weather, it's a beautiful place to enjoy afternoon beers and dinner. An older, families-with-kids crowd fills the space in daylight, with younger Staten Islanders rolling in as night falls.

I lean with the former group. What's better than a little day drinking in a German beer garden, with all that fresh air, *Gemütlichkeit*, sunshine, and trees? Not to mention Fräuleins bearing steins of twelve lively German brews on tap and fine food like sauerbraten, goulash, *und* schnitzel? Nothing. There is nothing better than that. Believe me—I've done the research. Just have a designated driver lined up, *meine Liebchen*.

THE FRONT WALKWAY AT KILLMEYER'S IS PAVED with BRICKS FIRED in the MID-1800S at BALTHASAR KREISCHER'S OLD NEW YORK FIRE BRICK AND STATEN ISLAND CLAY RETORT WORKS FACTORY, JUST DOWN THE STREET. YOU'LL SEE KREISCHER'S NAME on THOSE BRICKS AS YOU WALK INTO KILLMEYER'S TODAY.

KILLMEYER'S OLD BAVARIA INN

WHEN <u>TO</u> GO	Sunday afternoons, when the house oom-pah combo, the Happy Tones, oomp it up. *Happy hour: Monday to Friday, 4 to 7 p.m. Half-price select draft beers and $4 select wines and cocktails. Killmeyer's also runs happy hour specials on hearty bar food like potato pancakes, bratwurst, hoagies, and sliders.*
WHERE <u>TO</u> SIT	Weather permitting, out in the beer garden. Anywhere.
WHAT <u>TO</u> DRINK	Start with a Spaten lager, the top-seller at Killmeyer's. It's an excellent, classic German beer from Munich, which, Tirado says, "all the Heineken/Amstel people go for once they've tried it." Have room for another half liter? Get a Hefeweizen, the yeasty, south German style of wheat beer. Killmeyer's will always have a good one or three on tap, and they pair perfectly with warm weather and a little oom-pah.
HOW <u>TO</u> GET THERE	Killmeyer's is in deep southwest Staten Island, so your best bet is to drive or take a car service.
WHAT ELSE?	And take a gander at the giant Hummel figurine out front. He stands before Killmeyer's, midstride, in an impossible state of perpetual yodel. He's based on the German tchotchke manufacturer Hummel's "Merry Wanderer," and is indeed the world's largest Teutonic vaga-bond urchin, built in Cologne in the mid-seventies. He made it, all four thousand pounds of him (or 1,814 kilograms when he left Europe), to the New Jersey import company that then handled Hummel products. Eventually they went bankrupt and approached Tirado. "I guess they'd run out of ideas on what to do with the statue—I assume they tried to sell it first—when I got a phone call asking if I wanted it," he says. "I had to have it professionally moved, plus I had to have a steel-reinforced platform poured to support it."

LEE'S TAVERN

60 Hancock Street (at Garretson Avenue)   DONGAN HILLS, STATEN ISLAND
718-667-9749

THERE'S NO SIGN OUT FRONT AT LEE'S TAVERN, at the quiet corner where Staten Island's Hancock and Garretson intersect. They don't need one. Leroy Moresco opened it back in 1940, and everyone knows what it is: the local tavern in residential Dongan Hills, where everyone's gone since they were kids. It's a family-friendly place, specializing in what may be the best pizza on Staten Island, if not all of New York City. I do not say this lightly. This pizza is good. *So* damn—

"You can't curse here," says owner Diego Palemine, who took over the operation after his mom and dad passed on. "We don't allow cursing. We have families here." And why would you curse? The place is great. It's a cozy corner tavern with excellent food and an atmosphere of laid-back good cheer, loaded with life and light from the huge windows that flank the entrance.

Walk in, and it sounds like fun and smells like pizza. Pizza loaded with tangy red sauce, fennel-y sausage, and fresh mozzarella. There might be a game on the TV above the bar, but mostly you hear the voices: people laughing, greeting each other with big, back-slapping hugs, asking each other about their moms, their kids, their aunt—and how's she *doin'*, by the way? Beyond the smallish bar in front you'll find a couple dining rooms with photos of Dongan Hillers on the walls—firemen, cops, softball teams—and plaques and trophies from past touch-tackle football championships. Come in for the first time, and leave feeling like a local, too. "Even if you don't know someone you see here, you *feel* like you know 'em," Palemine says.

In 1969 Palemine's dad, Diego Sr., who'd worked there for years, bought Lee's from Moresco for a dollar, on one condition—that Moresco could continue working at Lee's as long as he wanted. That turned out to be a few more years, one or two days a week, before he died. Back then, young Diego worked there, too, "doin' everything—bussin' tables, washin' dishes, cleanin' up." In 2000 he got a gig at a restaurant in Manhattan's Waldorf Astoria hotel, but after 9/11, business fell way off. Normally at 110 percent capacity during the fall, that year the Waldorf was at about 2 percent, the guests all workers at Ground Zero. Palemine was laid off in October and came back to run the family business. But it turned out okay. He loves Lee's and it shows.

"It makes me happy to think that four generations, five generations of people want to come here," he says. "It makes me very happy." It'll make you happy, too.

On our first visit, with our friends Juan and Tony, we ordered a round of Coors Light and asked the big, no-nonsense bartender, John Connolly, for a pizza recommendation. No hesitation: sausage, garlic,

SPEAKING of THEIR PIZZA, THEIR WHITE CLAM PIE IS LEGENDARY,
NAMED A COUPLE OF TIMES in the *DAILY MEAL'S* "101 BEST PIZZAS IN AMERICA" LIST.
IT'S NOT YOUR TYPICAL HUGE, FLOPPY NEW YORK PIZZA. LEE'S SPECIALIZES in
STATEN ISLAND–STYLE "BAR PIZZA," SMALLER, THINNER-CRUSTED, AND CRISPIER THAN THE
STANDARD NEW YORK CITY PIE, and WORTH THE TRIP to LEE'S, WHEREVER YOU LIVE.

LEE'S TAVERN

and mozzarella. "Yeah, that'd be John," Palemine said. "That's *his* pizza." Diego goes for the chicken and hot peppers. Everyone has "their pizza" at Lee's.

We demolished our pie and ordered more cold beers. Juan took a satisfied look around and smiled: "I love a bar with a couple of old guys hanging out in the corner." Me too. "I like it," he proclaimed. "This place is attitude-free, comfortable, and welcoming."

"You come in here and you relax," says Diego. "You don't have to be anyone else. It's a judgment-free zone. You'll get a politician sitting next to a plumber sitting next to a doctor sitting next to a city worker. It's just a real good cross section of life."

WHEN TO GO	Late afternoon on a Saturday or Sunday. Hang out at the bar when the place is mellow and watch a little sportsball on TV. ("We're a little more Mets/Giants/Rangers than Yankees/Jets/Devils," says Diego.) Have a couple drinks and order a pizza. Make it *your* pizza. Want to see Lee's in all its local glory? Stick around as the neighbors descend on the place at dinnertime.
WHERE TO SIT	The front of the bar, to your right as you walk in, next to the windows facing Garretson. "You can see everything that happens around the block," says Palemine. "Not that much is ever really *happening*, but . . ."
WHAT TO DRINK	Start out with a Coors Light, their best seller. It pairs perfectly with pizza. Next get whatever Flagship beer they have on tap. It'll be delicious and fresh, as it's brewed nearby, right on Staten Island.
HOW TO GET THERE	The Staten Island Railway stops a block away at the Dongan Hills Station. You can pick up the train near the ferry dock on the island's north end. And, of course, you can drive to Lee's by way of the mighty Verrazano-Narrows Bridge.
WHAT ELSE?	Lee's stocks the absolute best sausage I've had on a pizza in New York City. I raved about it to Palemine and he said, "Thank you very much. I appreciate that. It's a proprietary blend made for us by Arrochar Meats, a local butcher down the block." Hats off to Arrochar. They nailed it. It's crumbly, rich, and loaded with fennel and spices, head and shoulders above the pedestrian sliced sausage you find on too many New York pies.

LIEDY'S SHORE INN

748 Richmond Terrace (between Clinton and Lafayette Avenues)   NEW BRIGHTON, STATEN ISLAND
718-447-9240

THE SECOND YOU STEP INTO LIEDY'S SHORE INN, you know you're someplace historic. Look up at that old, pressed-tin ceiling. Smell the wood of the oak bar and the building itself, which looks from the outside like a tidy residential row house with a saloon surgically attached at the bottom. Just yards away from the Kill Van Kull waterway, this is a waterfront bar, and has been for a very long time, and when the brackish breeze from the harbor blows in, you're reminded of the Shore Inn's waterfront past.

It's a hyper-local bar, fiercely embraced by its clientele, many from the surrounding New Brighton neighborhood. The regular crowd is mostly over fifty, and you'll see a few of these patrons hanging out indoors on quiet afternoons, or sometimes sitting in lawn chairs on the sidewalk out front when the weather is mild. The owner, Larry Liedy, keeps the place going, and the regulars love him for that.

His great-grandpa, Jacob Liedy, founded the bar back in 1905, when the neighborhood was bustling with shipping, factories, and a gypsum plant. Business moved away and the neighborhood slowed down, but Liedy's kept on going. Larry inherited the Shore Inn from his dad in 1990, making it the oldest family-run bar on the island.

It's peaceful during the day, a pleasant spot to enjoy a relaxing beer with friends and maybe watch a game on TV. On nights when a band is playing, everything changes. Liedy's flips from a sleepy neighborhood bar to a rowdy middle-aged dance party. Live bands pound out classic rock covers, the place is packed, drinks flow, and everyone's moving, laughing, yelling, loving it. It's like a forty-year class reunion (with a few younger folks crashing the party), the old gang slamming beers, cutting loose, and carrying on *hard*, backed by the soundtrack of youth, with the inevitable flirting, razzing, and bullshitting that goes with it. People drift out front, some with their drinks, smoking, howling, mopping their brows. Guys in trucks and cars pull up to the curb, like Wooderson in *Dazed and Confused*, chatting up the ladies, breaking balls. Don't bother calling the cops. Some are already here, along with firefighters, teachers, and sanitation workers. It's a Staten Island scene.

Our friend Tony, who grew up nearby, looked around wistfully during a thirst-driven crush at the bar between sets, smiled, and said, "I remember when *all* Staten Island bars used to have live music." On Wednesdays, Fridays, and Saturdays, this one still does, with Larry Liedy himself occasionally manning a guitar.

WHEN TO GO	Friday or Saturday night, for the party.
WHERE TO SIT	You're not going to sit, hombre, you're going to *dance*. If you must sit and cool off, grab a lawn chair out front, unless the regulars beat you to 'em.
WHAT TO DRINK	Beer. Whiskey. Repeat.
HOW TO GET THERE	Liedy's is on the north shore of Staten Island, where there is no train. You can take a quick bus ride on the S40 or S44 from the ferry to Lafayette Avenue. Another option: take a cab or car service. Make sure someone else is driving you home, bud.
WHAT ELSE?	For decades Liedy's was home base to a group of old men known as "the Snugs," who lived just up the street. The Snugs were retired seamen from Sailors' Snug Harbor, a sprawling campus for "aged, decrepit, and worn-out" merchant seamen founded by Revolutionary War veteran Robert Richard Randall. It was grand, a stately collection of twenty-six Greek Revival, Victorian, and Italianate buildings on rolling, manicured lawns. Eventually it fell into disrepair, and by the seventies the whole operation moved to North Carolina. Many of the remaining buildings attained landmark status, avoiding demolition, and the campus is now part of the Snug Harbor Cultural Center and Botanical Garden. But for years, as Larry Liedy can tell you, those old sailors would drift a couple blocks up Richmond Terrace and into the Shore, where they would drink away their days and tell the best stories a kid would ever want to hear.

WHICH is the OLDEST BAR on STATEN ISLAND, KILLMEYER'S or LIEDY'S? ACCORDING to SILIVE.COM, THE SHORE INN, HAVING OPENED IN 1905 AND BEEN RUN by the LIEDY FAMILY EVER SINCE, IS "THE OLDEST CONTINUOUSLY RUN BAR STILL in OPERATION ON STATEN ISLAND." KILLMEYER'S, in a BUILDING DATING TO 1859, IS "ARGUABLY the OLDEST STRUCTURE THAT HOUSES A BAR on STATEN ISLAND."

THE LONG ISLAND BAR

110 Atlantic Avenue (at Henry Street) COBBLE HILL, BROOKLYN
thelongislandbar.com · *718-625-8908*

IN 1951, RAMON MONTERO OPENED the Long Island Bar & Restaurant on Atlantic Avenue, a few blocks from New York Harbor. It was an unpretentious spot, serving neighbors, dockworkers, and folks from nearby Long Island College Hospital. Ramon's daughter Emma and her husband, Buddy Sullivan, took over in 1956 and ran the Long Island with help from Emma's cousins Pepita and Maruja. Buddy died in 1977, but the ladies continued on until Emma decided to move back to her native Spain, and one night in 2007, the staff cleaned the bar, put the chairs up, and closed the place—and it stayed that way until 2013.

Joel Tompkins and Toby Cecchini saw the beauty in this abandoned gem and tried for months to get a meeting to discuss a lease. After sliding many notes under the door to no avail, a chance encounter with a relative of the owners led to success in 2013. They promised not to change a thing, signed the lease, polished her up, and opened a gateway to the past.

"This place was an icon in the neighborhood for sixty years," says Cecchini, "and ironically played a big role during its closed years" because so many people in the community speculated on the Long Island's fate during its closure. As the neighborhood was swept up in Brooklyn's frenzied Manhattanization, Cecchini thought surely "some clown would turn it into a bank." Instead, he and Tompkins opened an old-fashioned neighborhood tavern, a gathering spot reminiscent of the kind Cecchini grew up with in Eau Claire, Wisconsin. "We preserved every iota we could," Cecchini says. "People say over and over, 'Bless you for keeping this place the way it was.' We kept it intact."

Neighbors responded enthusiastically to this rescue, and it's become a vibrant social hub again. "It's like an extension of my living room," says Cam Dale, who lives next door to the Long Island and has tended bar there. "I go there to seek people out, watch the games. It's the heart of the neighborhood."

And it's only getting better—and buzzier. The Long Island is as good for dinner with the family as it is for drinks with friends after work. The food menu is succinct and strong. You can enjoy a dinner of grilled trout, brown butter gnocchi, clams, or a mighty fine hamburger and fries in the "Sinatra Booth," or pitchers of Kölsch and fried cheese curds (Wisconsin-style, only lighter and tastier, according to experts from the Badger State) back in the cozy Lombardi Room.

THE SLEEK, ART DECO–ERA BAR WAS BUILT BY HAND IN 1949 BY RAMON MONTERO. THE EDGES of the BAR, ESPECIALLY on the SHORT END NEAR the FRONT, ARE BRANDED with BLACK SCARS WHERE BUDDY SULLIVAN'S YEARS of FORGOTTEN CIGARETTES BURNED THE WOOD. TOMPKINS and CECCHINI INTENTIONALLY PRESERVED THOSE VINTAGE POCKMARKS, VARNISHING THEM to a DEEP SHEEN.

THE LIGHT SCONCES OVER THE BOOTHS? THE ORIGINALS WERE LONG GONE WHEN TOMPKINS *and* CECCHINI TOOK OVER, SO THESE WERE MADE-TO-ORDER BASED *on a* 1950S-ERA LIGHTOLIER SCONCE TOMPKINS FOUND *on* EBAY. THE LITTLE PULL CHAINS *are* THERE *for* SHOW ONLY. THE LIGHTS ARE CONTROLLED *with a* WALL SWITCH BEHIND THE BAR, SO DON'T BOTHER PLAYING WITH 'EM.

WHEN TO GO	Early evening. The Long Island opens daily at 5:30 p.m., and if you get there before the dinner rush, you'll have as perfect a cocktail hour as you could ever hope for. Or, for a rowdy good time, join Wisconsin ex-pats in the Lombardi Room for a Green Bay Packers game.
WHERE TO SIT	Cecchini says it's the westernmost stool at the bar, past the elbow and against the wall, and I agree. The Long Island is my local bar, and that's my favorite spot. There, a patron is nicely tucked in, away from floor traffic, with a wall of north-facing windows on one side and a view of the entire bar on the other.
WHAT TO DRINK	Most popular: the Long Island Gimlet, made with gin and homemade lime-ginger cordial. Not to be missed: the Boulevardier, pronounced "boo-luh-VAR-dee-ay." It means, literally, a guy who walks the boule-vards. A man about town. *C'est français.*

HOUSE RECIPES

The Boulevardier

1 ounce Rittenhouse rye
1 ounce Old Overholt rye
1 ounce house sweet vermouth
(2 parts Cinzano Rosso to 1 part Carpano Antica Formula)
1 ounce Campari

Stir all the ingredients with ice in a large mixing glass, allowing for "respectable dilution." Strain into a chilled coupe glass and garnish with a lemon twist.

The L.I.B. Gimlet

2 ounces gin
1 ounce lime-ginger cordial
¾ ounce fresh lime juice

Shake all the ingredients in a cocktail shaker with ice and strain into a double old-fashioned glass with ice. Garnish with two lime wheels.

Bonus: Order a cosmopolitan from Cecchini and his brow may furrow slightly. While working at Tribeca's fabled Odeon bar in the eighties, he perfected and popularized the signature pink drink of the *Sex and the City* years, a perfectly good cocktail made poorly by legions of bartenders since, a burden he must carry like an "albatross around [his] neck" for the rest of his life. Order one anyway. It's as fun to drink as it is to watch Cecchini dolefully—and perfectly—prepare it.

HOW <u>TO</u> GET THERE

The Borough Hall subway station, a major Brooklyn travel hub and stop for the 2/3, 4/5, and R trains, is only a ten-minute walk away, as is the F/G stop on Bergen Street, a few blocks to LIB's east.

WHAT ELSE?

Notice the blue neon NO DANCING sign at the far end of the front room (it features in many an Instagram post, often with *Footloose* references), a round Julio Iglesias photo by the cash register (younger patrons always ask, "Who's *that* guy?"), and the hubba-hubba ceramic lamp to the register's left, for which Cecchini was once offered five thousand dollars. (He couldn't sell it. Ask him why.)

LUCKYDOG

303 Bedford Avenue (between South Second and South First Streets)   WILLIAMSBURG, BROOKLYN
No phone. "If you left your credit card, come back to the bar.
If you lost your scarf, come back to the bar. We don't take reservations. Just come to the bar."

LUCKYDOG IS, FIRST AND FOREMOST, A NEIGHBORHOOD DIVE BAR (the good kind, not the sad, broken-down kind), known for its on-point music, great beers, and love of dogs. The bar's namesake, Lucky, was owner Sal Fristensky's old pooch, and to this day people from all over Brooklyn stop by with their dogs and hang out for a while.

Located on a quieter part of Williamsburg's Bedford Avenue, the place gives off an unpolished, comfortable vibe. It feels a little don't-give-a-shit punkish at first: some of the staff legendarily wear black BRUNCH IS FOR ASSHOLES T-shirts, a jokey jab at this brunch-crazed neighborhood. Scruffy regulars roll in shortly after noon, sliding onto their favorite stools for whiskey and/or beer. At first glance you might take Luckydog for just another dive with 'tude and move along, but sit, boy. Sit. Hang out for a few minutes, and you'll see that this place is good. *It's a GOOD bar! Who's a GOOD bar? YOU are, Luckydog! YOU are!*

Much of that is thanks to owners Fristensky and Bill Mack, who nail the basics, those things bartender Melissa Spalding calls "the unnoticeables that make a bar so good: the light and sound level, the height of the bar stools, the rail, the bar itself. They dialed it in." The beer-loving staff makes the place even better, handling their jobs with an unfussy grace that quickly puts folks at ease.

And Luckydog's selection of craft beers is excellent, with twenty brews on tap, including quality oddballs and special releases that, according to bartender Sean Caffrey, "beer nerds come from all over to drink." Consider the outstanding house brew: Bill and Sal's Excellent Adventure, an IPA made by the Bronx Brewery exclusively for Luckydog's owners. "It's an unfiltered, seven percent ABV, dank-weed IPA," says Mack. "This beer is brewed and kegged in the South Bronx, then shipped to Brooklyn, direct to our bar." Luckydog also sells a couple cheap beers by the pitcher. Can I get a *hells yeah?*

It's the kind of place where you want to hang out for a while and shoot the shit. The music is good. The bartenders are easy to talk to and so are the patrons. There's pinball *and* a shuffleboard table, both very popular with the kids, and a clean backyard patio. It all works, and the regulars agree. One bearded fellow I talked to found his local at Luckydog before he even found his apartment. "They're welcoming to everybody, and the service is always amazing," he said. "It's like their living room," Spalding added, pointing to the locals at the bar. "More like our *family* room," the guy corrected.

THE OLD CD JUKEBOX (A SOLID MIX of COUNTRY, ROCK AND ROLL, HAIR METAL, and BLUES) IS CONSIDERED ONE of the BEST IN NEW YORK CITY, and THE BARTENDERS' PLAYLISTS ARE NO SLOUCH EITHER. ON ONE VISIT I HEARD EMMYLOU HARRIS, SUPERTRAMP, GEORGE JONES, THE ALLMAN BROTHERS, CHUCK BERRY, DOLLY PARTON, HOYT AXTON, BOB DYLAN, BUDDY GUY, AND JOHNNY CASH, IN THAT ORDER.

WHEN TO GO	Saturday or Sunday, early afternoon, when there's a mix of regulars and visitors, the sun is shining, and Luckydog puts out free, fresh bagels and cream cheese from Bagelsmith down the street.
	Happy hour: Monday to Friday, noon to 7 p.m. $1 off pints of draft beer; $3 well drinks; $2 PBR and Schaefer cans; $3 bottles of Miller High Life and Lone Star.
WHERE TO SIT	Anywhere out on the back patio, if weather permits. There, on a beautiful June afternoon, I met a friendly Boston terrier hanging out with his people. I'm told it's illegal in New York to ask whether or not he was a service dog, but I *do* know he was a *lucky* dog.
WHAT TO DRINK	Pick a beer, any beer. You will always get a clean, fresh pour. (Every draft line is cleaned regularly as a point of pride.) Ask for a taste of something unusual, and the bartender will be happy to oblige you. Not into beer? Have the popular One-Pound Margarita. (Not that anyone's actually *weighed* it, but hey. Don't lay a *literalist* trip on Luckydog, man.)
HOUSE RECIPE	**Luckydog One-Pound Margarita**

2 ounces Rancho Alegre tequila blanco
1 ounce Cointreau
1 ounce house-made sour mix (recipe follows)

Shake all the ingredients in a cocktail shaker loaded with ice. Strain over fresh ice into a mason jar with a salted rim and garnish with a lime wedge.

Luckydog Sour Mix

2 parts simple syrup (equal parts water and sugar, stirred or shaken until the sugar completely dissolves)

1 part fresh lime juice
1 part fresh lemon juice

HOW TO GET THERE

Subway: The L train stops just up the street at Bedford Avenue.

WHAT ELSE?

Behind the bar at Luckydog you'll see a wondrous sight: the fullest array of Louisiana's Zapp's brand potato chips outside of Parasol's Bar in New Orleans. This may be the greatest beer bar snack in the known universe (back off; I've done the research), with flavors ranging from Spicy Cajun Crawtator to Hotter 'n Hot Jalapeño. But beyond Zapp's and the occasional free weekend bagel, Luckydog doesn't serve food. If you need chow, don't worry. You're in Williamsburg, with about thirty-five thousand options for excellent eats. Borrow a menu from the bartenders' stash, or Google whatever your heart desires. Order pickup or delivery, then dine right there at the bar or out on the back patio.

Luckydog was an early adopter of the "funny chalkboard" trend, and they're pretty good at it. "Every shift, a bartender will write something witty on the chalkboard," Spalding told me. "For example: 'Forecast: Heavy Pours,' 'Walk of Shame Checkpoint,' 'Take a Trip to the Spirit World,' 'Brunch Is for Assholes,' etc. Our bartenders and their personalities are a big part of the bar." That's Luckydog, and as Sam Jackson said in *Pulp Fiction*, "A *dog* has personality, and *personality* goes a long way."

McSORLEY'S
OLD ALE HOUSE

15 East Seventh Street (between Second and Third Avenues)   EAST VILLAGE, MANHATTAN
mcsorleysoldalehouse.nyc   ·   *212-473-9148*

McSORLEY'S IS THE GRANDDADDY of New York City's Irish bars. It smells old and woody and beery and historic. It's been in the same spot on Seventh Street since 1854, and looking at the walls, you'll believe it. The place is practically a museum that serves beer. And that, by the way, is your only beverage option, so get on board and order them in even numbers, because they're sold two at a time, in sturdy mugs that hold around eight and a half ounces.

Weekday afternoons at McSorley's are about as good as it gets: peaceful and light-filled, with plenty of elbow room to move around freely and check out the artifacts covering the walls. You'll probably find a seat during the off hours. If there's room at one of the already-occupied round tables, grab a chair. That's fine, even encouraged—it's a chatty bar, so you'll likely get into an interesting conversation. But the solitary reader has a place at McSorley's, and writers, too. Owner Mattie Maher warns that "when you start comin' here, you don't stop writin'."

Maher, a native of Kilkenny, Ireland, began working at McSorley's in 1964, when he stumbled into a server's job because the *other* Irish guy who'd just been hired hadn't shown up for his first shift. The bartender on duty threw an apron at Maher and barked, "You're late," and the rest is history. He started that day and never looked back. Now he's the boss. The owner at the time, Daniel Kirwan, asked him to buy the bar in 1977—"The original family was gone, and there was nobody left." You might find Maher's daughter and heir apparent, Teresa, working the bar these days, a far cry from the time not that long ago when it was a hard-drinking saloon that allowed only men. (That changed in 1970.)

McSorley's leads a sort of double life. Even though it's in all the guidebooks and sought out by a million tourists, it's still—much of the time—a perfectly gorgeous, quiet old bar for drinking up beer (and history) and talking with friends and strangers. There's something fantastically convivial about the place, maybe due to more than sixteen decades of pubby good cheer, camaraderie, and conversation, which have saturated the walls and the wood like long-gone cigar smoke. At its heart, McSorley's is a talkin' bar. You might meet a PhD candidate who can enlighten you on Thomas Wolfe's literary oeuvre or a world-weary NBC cameraman who was at Ground Zero on 9/11. (I've encountered both.) Other times, especially on weekends and around the holidays, it may be jam-packed with a crush of college

kids and out-of-towners, which, if you're in the mood, can be a blast. (If you're *not* in the mood, less so.) As a rule, though, the crowd, young and old, local or not, is boisterous, chatty, and having a great time.

Anyone who writes off McSorley's for its crowds is throwing the baby out with the bathwater, like people who discredit the Beatles because they don't like "I Want to Hold Your Hand." Legendary *New Yorker* staff writer Joe Mitchell, who wrote a sprawling, classic paean to McSorley's back in 1940, was no fool. It's in the pantheon of great American bars for a reason.

McSorley's leads a sort OF double life. Even though it's in all the guidebooks and sought out by a million tourists, it's still—much of the time— a perfectly gorgeous, quiet, old bar FOR drinking up beer (and history) and talking with friends and strangers.

WHEN TO GO

McSorley's is wildly popular with both tourists and the neighborhood's huge New York University student population, so crowds can be thick on weekend evenings. If a crowd isn't what you're feeling, visit afternoons and weekday evenings, when the bar is more likely to be chill.

WHERE TO SIT

"When it's busy, *any* seat," according to Maher; the tables next to the front, south-facing windows are especially good. John Lennon was a regular in the seventies, and favored the seat to the left of the front door, where he could hang out on quiet afternoons and "do a little writin'." Maher once struck up a conversation with Lennon and discovered they'd met several times as kids in Maher's hometown of Kilkenny. He remembers playing with Lennon—"just a regular kid"—on the streets near Lennon's uncle's drapery shop.

WHAT TO DRINK

Ale or porter, sold by the pair and brewed by the Lion Brewery in Wilkes-Barre, Pennsylvania. Drink 'em up and order another even-numbered round. That's what you're there for. Fun fact: The bottled version of McSorley's beer (sold nationally) features a portrait on the label of old John McSorley himself by master caricaturist Drew Friedman, who was paid in—you guessed it—beer.

WHAT ELSE?

Where to start? The wishbones balanced precariously on the gas lamp above the bar since—legend has it—World War I. On the walls, Victorian-era photos of the bar's former baseball team, the McSorley's Nine, handlebar mustaches and all; dozens of framed front pages from long-defunct newspapers and political posters; a 1943 photo of Woody Guthrie playing for the workingmen by the potbelly stove (still used in cooler months, by the way); a wanted poster of John Wilkes Booth. There's an enormous "collage" installation of old stuff behind the bar: a shot of Babe Ruth before his final at bat, campaign buttons (Nixon, Kennedy—both John and Ted—others indiscernible), Purple Hearts, a bust of JFK sporting a pair of cheap sunglasses, and, on occasion, a Yankees cap. Flags (mostly Irish and American); figurines (a racehorse, a corny leprechaun, a Statue of Liberty); pewter and brass tankards, ceramic mugs, bottles, bottles, and more bottles (all shrouded in dust); stashes of receipts for God-knows-what; a carving warning patrons to "Be Good or Be Gone"; masks, pipes, canes, mounted fish. Sailor hats, soldier hats, Santa hats. A nineteenth-century "What? Me worry?" picture featuring the jug-eared, dentally challenged goofball who would later inspire *Mad*'s Alfred E. Neuman. Feast your eyes. Notice every-thing you can.

THE BAR ITSELF WAS CRAFTED *in* 1854 OUT OF OAK, SAYS MAHER. IT'S A STANDING BAR, WITH NO STOOLS, JUST A LONG FOOTRAIL. GOOGLE AN IMAGE OF ARTIST JOHN SLOAN'S FAMOUS 1912 PAINTING *McSORLEY'S BAR*, NOW HANGING *in the* DETROIT INSTITUTE OF ARTS. IT LOOKS PRETTY MUCH THE SAME IN THAT PAINTING AS IT DOES TODAY.

MONA'S

224 Avenue B (between East Thirteenth and East Fourteenth Streets)   EAST VILLAGE, MANHATTAN
212-353-3780

MONA'S IS A TEXTBOOK EXAMPLE of an old New York dive bar, with the no-frills decor, local barflies, and cheap drinks to earn the distinction. Rich Corton, who owns the place with Kirk Marcoe, says the principles behind Mona's are "cheap-priced beer and alcohol, good rock and roll on the juke, and a pool table. *And* it's non-exclusionary." That pretty much sums up the perfect dive right there.

Mona's divey bona fides are in order. It's a great place to get back to the basics in a neighborhood that's changed dramatically since the bar opened in 1989. But New York dives, good and bad, are a dime a dozen, despite all those that have disappeared lately because of rent increases, building sales, and attrition.

What sets Mona's apart is the music. It's home base to a couple of die-hard communities of musicians and their fans, who descend like pigeons on bread crumbs every Monday and Tuesday night.

Mondays are for bluegrass, when guitarist Rick Snell hosts his open session featuring Appalachian fiddle music, bluegrass, and old-school country. Devotees of Bill Monroe, the Stanley Brothers, Flatt, Fleck, Scruggs, and Skaggs converge weekly around 9:30 p.m. to pick, grin, hoot, and/or holler till the moon is o'er the mountain. You'll see many of the same faces week after week, and new ones popping in now and again, adding to the circle. And these people jam, hard.

Tuesday nights from eleven on are for old-timey jazz, the traditional stuff that flowered in New Orleans in the early nineteen hundreds, moved up the river to St. Louis and Chicago, then hopped over to New York and Europe in the twenties. *Hot* jazz. Think Louis Armstrong, Jelly Roll Morton, and Sidney Bechet. Bouncy music with a syncopated swing, heavy on brass, clarinet, upright bass, and piano. We're talking the kind of lively jazz you'd hear in a wacky Woody Allen "caper" scene, not the abstract *squonk* jazz of the late fifties that sounded like a nightmare soundtrack for Hollywood's idea of a heroin trip, and definitely not "the *smooth jazz* of the seventies, eighties, and today" that you hear on lame radio stations.

Tuesday-night jazz has become quite a thing at Mona's since Dennis Lichtman got it going in 2007. At first it was just a few musicians showing up after nearby gigs to jam, with a handful of people in the bar listening. But the timing was significant. The trad jazz scene was bubbling up in New York around then, with younger people getting into it, both as musicians and listeners.

Now Lichtman and Mona's Hot Four (as the core group is called) play from eleven to midnight as the crowd builds, then open up the jam to other musicians, some of whom show up in coats and ties

and dresses and even tuxedos after gigs with the likes of Vince Giordano's Nighthawks at Iguana on Fifty-fourth Street. Sometimes up to thirty musicians will cycle through during a session, joining the circle for a while before heading home. The jam lasts until around three in the morning. "It's been ruining my Wednesdays for a while, man," Lichtman jokes. "I don't plan anything too early on Wednesdays."

It's been ruining a lot of Wednesdays, judging from the crowds. Sometimes over the course of a session as many as two hundred folks show up to listen, and some come almost every week. "It's absolutely a community on its own," Lichtman says, and it shows no sign of slowing down.

"At first we just did it to have a good time and a few free beers," says Lichtman. "We never expected it to get so big. We'll do it as long as it's vibrant and still feels like a community."

If bluegrass or early jazz stirs your soul, makes your heart sing, or at the very least gets your toes a-tappin', follow your bliss and head down to Mona's on Monday or Tuesday night to meet up with your tribe. Mona's is about "community," says Corton. "It's the neighborhood and people that come in and have created a convivial, friendly atmosphere here, open to anyone."

What sets Mona's apart is THE music. It's home base TO A couple of die-hard communities of musicians and their fans, who descend like pigeons ON bread crumbs every Monday and Tuesday night.

WHEN TO GO	Into bluegrass? Stop by between 9:30 p.m. and midnight or so on Mondays. Traditional jazz? Then Tuesdays at eleven are for you, and the fun runs till "stupid late."
WHERE TO SIT	Seat, schmeat. You're gonna stand, my friend. It's gonna be tight in there, so grab a cold drink, scooch in as close to the clutch of musicians as you can, and get cozy with your neighbors.

WHAT *TO* DRINK

A pint of Guinness, "recognized as one of the best in the city," according to Corton. Then, water. Good old H-two-O. It's late, it's crowded, you've already been drinking, you have to work tomorrow, and, really, you've *got* to stay hydrated. Don't *ruin your Wednesday*.

HOW *TO* GET THERE

Subway: The L train stops at 1st Avenue and 14th Street, just two blocks west of Mona's.

WHAT ELSE?

Who the heck *is* Mona, the bar's namesake? Mona was the cat of the original owner, Richard Corton's brother Bob.

Oh, how the East Village has changed. Back in 1989 when Mona's first opened, the neighborhood was practically an open-air drug market, the Marrakesh of smack, coke, and crack. "For example," Corton says, "the space next to what is now Subway [at 223 Avenue B, across the street from Mona's] was a 'deli,' but in name only, because all they would sell you was drugs. You would walk in and the counter was behind bullet-proof glass. You simply asked for drugs and they would sell to you. People coming and going from the bar were routinely mugged, including myself." And that's the way it was in pre-Giuliani New York City, children, for better or for worse, depending on whom you ask.

A few surprising musicians have sat in on these sessions, among them Jon Batiste, leader of Stay Human, the house band for *The Late Show with Stephen Colbert*. "We've gotten some older musicians, too," says Lichtman. "People who used to play with Benny Goodman and people like that."

MONTERO BAR & GRILL

73 Atlantic Avenue (at Hicks Street) BROOKLYN HEIGHTS, BROOKLYN
646-729-4129

MONTERO'S IS ONE OF THOSE BARS THAT PEOPLE *LOVE*, the way people love *Star Wars* or the Beach Boys or a special birthday meal their mom cooked for them every year when they were kids. "Love" in a deep, heartfelt, nostalgic way. I get it. It's a special place. In the late afternoon it can be peaceful, calm, and timeless, like the attic of a hundred-year-old brownstone. Slide onto a seat at the bar and take it in.

Visually, there's *a lot* to take in, too, but it's not jarring. It's intentional, well tended, and really quite beautiful, especially when you consider that this was a no-frills, workingman's waterfront dive for most of its history. Montero's is like a full-scale folk art diorama, crafted over decades by a collective of working-class seafaring artisans, all lovingly maintained by owner Pepe Montero's wife, Linda, who keeps the place clean, tidy, and true to form.

Their fine old Corvin neon sign outside foreshadows good stuff within. The front room holds a modest bar topped with orangey-red Formica echoing the color of the seven authentic life preservers that hang above, spray-painted with names and ports like S.T. Charleston N.Y., T.B. New Jersey Wilmington Del., and Edward Rutledge New York N.Y. You'll notice two thirties-era Bell telephone booths—the indoor kind, bulky and woody, with glass-paned privacy doors—and a working triple-expansion steam engine a little farther back.

Wood paneling covers the walls, real wood the color of dark chocolate, seasoned by the smoke from a million cigarettes and mounted with photos, portraits of ships, and posters like the Spanish one touting bullfights featuring "Juan H. Garcia, El Califa" and "Jesus Iglesias, El Campesino." There are nautical-themed timepieces, carved figurines of assorted salty dogs, and lanterns, hats, caps, flags, and flying machines of all kinds hanging from the ceiling. Look for five portholes—thick, heavy, brass-and-glass suckers—gifted by three different sailors, several bells, and more model ships than I wanted to count, including a massive one of the *Cutty Sark* in a case above the front door. She was an 1869 British clipper, *yar*, one of the fastest and most famous ships in the world, her name lifted from Robert Burns's 1790 poem *Tam o' Shanter*, wherein is described one beguilingly beautiful witch, Nannie Dee, who, during some late-night witchery, is spied wearing a sinfully delicious short chemise, a *cutty-sark* in Scottish, and, well . . . it goes on. You can see where a good docent like Pepe adds to the Montero experience.

A lot of the stuff at Montero's was bequeathed by the seamen who ate, drank, bird-dogged, cashed their paychecks, and beat each other up there. They had a strong connection to the place not only

AFTER HE SPLIT with HIS FIRST WIFE IN 1979, *ANGELA'S ASHES* AUTHOR FRANK McCOURT LIVED in the APARTMENT ABOVE MONTERO'S, RECOUNTING IN HIS MEMOIR *TEACHER MAN* THAT "OUTSIDE MY WINDOW, THE MONTERO BAR NEON SIGN BLAZED ON AND OFF, TURNING MY FRONT ROOM FROM SCARLET TO BLACK TO SCARLET WHILE on the JUKEBOX DOWNSTAIRS THE VILLAGE PEOPLE SANG AND POUNDED 'YMCA.'"

MONTERO BAR & GRILL

because it was close to the waterfront where they docked, but also because founder Joe Montero, Pepe's father, was a merchant marine himself. These were his people. He and his wife, Pilar, made them feel welcome for decades, and Pepe continued that tradition of hospitality after Joe gave him the bar. This adventuresome seafaring clientele of course led to a bunch of good stories, and I'll share one true tale from Pepe.

It was the late sixties, and the crews from a Greek ship and an Argentine ship, docked nearby, were drinking in Montero's. The ships' cooks started arguing about who made better food. Things got heated, and before they could start punching, Pepe suggested the obvious solution: a cook-off on the sidewalk in front of the bar. Well, the crews went back to their ships and returned with cooking supplies: grills, two industrial-size barbecue pits, heaps of beef and pork (the Greeks), and one entire steer (the Argentines). So much meat and gear that the contest extended right off the sidewalk and into westbound Atlantic Avenue.

The kitchen crews fired up their grills and started cooking, and soon the irresistible aroma of roasting beef and pork wafted eastward. Drooling Brooklynites from a half mile downwind began showing up at Montero's, drawn by their noses. Cops directed Atlantic Avenue traffic around the expanding competition. The crew of a Spanish ship docked nearby wanted in on the action and added a couple hundred pounds of sardines to the grills. Wine was drunk. Beer was drunk. Everyone was drunk. Dignitaries from the Argentine consulate showed up, tipped off by the sailors, and set up to dine on a white tablecloth inside. More people gathered, watching in anticipation, licking their chops like housecats hearing a can opening up.

The feast finally commenced. By the end of the night, more than three hundred people ate for free, a gift from the Argentines, Greeks, and Spaniards. And who won? Pepe waves off the question. "By the end of the night, after all that food and wine, they were all in love, the best of friends."

WHEN TO GO

Depends on what you want. Late afternoon, you'll have a nice, quiet experience, maybe with a middle-aged regular or two sipping a beer at the bar, discussing trivia and history, or maybe with an off-duty bartender from another neighborhood place (they tend to like Montero's) discussing the merits of ice-cold American macrobrews. You want a party? Stop by after ten on a Thursday, Friday, or Saturday night, when the joint is packed with a younger crowd for karaoke, and Montero's rocks till four, long after the sidewalks of Brooklyn Heights and Cobble Hill have been rolled up for the night.

WHERE TO SIT

The late matriarch Pilar Montero's favorite seat at the end of the bar to the left as you walk in, against the wall below the picture of her husband, Joe, and his ship, the USS *President Monroe*, where he served as chief engineer during World War II. She regularly held down that seat till she died in 2012, and there's a faded 1947 photo showing her in that very same spot the night Montero opened to prove it. It hangs in the porthole to the right of the door as you walk in.

WHAT TO DRINK

Most popular: a bottle of beer. No drafts, just ice-cold bottles. PBR and Bud are the top sellers. Next drink: a shot. You're at an old sailor bar, for the love o' Neptune. Pepe says, "The guys like Jameson's and the girls like Fireball."

HOW TO GET THERE

Subway: Take the 2, 3, 4 , or 5 to Borough Hall or the R to Court Street, all about a ten-minute walk away.

WHAT ELSE?

True story: It's about 1962 and a young Pepe Montero is cleaning up the bar before it opened for the day. A limo with a police escort pulls up, stops in front of the bar, and a guy in short sleeves gets out of the car. He's got tattoos all over his arms and chest, which Pepe could see peeking out from his open collar. Sailor tattoos. He comes in and asks for Pepe's dad, Joe. Says he heard from his friends in the Danish merchant marines that if he's ever in New York, he has to have a beer at Montero's. (The Danes really loved the place, as Joe Montero had shipped out with many of them in his seagoing days.) The man with the tattoos? King Frederick IX of Denmark, a former sailor with the ink to prove it.

Montero's is one of the few places that sells Pabst Blue Ribbon in bottles (as opposed to cans), and they sell a hell of a lot of them, along with bottles of Bud, Bud Light, Brooklyn Lager, and others. They prefer bottles to cans; the beer tastes better and stays cold longer. On the downside, they're much heavier. Fortunately, Montero's has a good old-fashioned dumbwaiter, one of a few still working in New York, and it is used to haul case after hefty case of those bottled suds up from storage in the basement.

MUGS ALEHOUSE

125 Bedford Avenue (at North Tenth Street) WILLIAMSBURG, BROOKLYN
mugsalehouse.com · 718-486-8232

MUGS CAME TO BE AT A PIVOTAL TIME in Williamsburg's history. It was 1992, and "definitely Hipsterville," as Mugs owner Ed Berestecki puts it, but not yet completely over-the-shark gentrified. There were local bars, sure, but none yet selling good craft beer, so Berestecki opened one up, and Mugs Alehouse was born.

The craft beer thing was starting to take off, and beer lovers came from all over New York to sample the goodies from Berestecki's sixteen, then twenty-four, *then* thirty-two taps (plus two casks). Thus, Mugs became one of the major hubs of the new craft beer scene. A genesis, of sorts. Berestecki said, "Let there be Beer." And it was good.

It's a first-wave craft beer bar of its era, the nineties, with all the requisite signs, neon, and banners. The crowd is a good-natured mix of local and visiting craft beer fans, and I like that kind of crowd. They're generally social, chatty, and happy to be there, enjoying the nectar they're knocking back, not just grimly putting it down like medicine. You see a lot of bellies and gray beards at Mugs, along with plenty of younger beer lovers, too, and a few Polish working-class guys from the neighborhood. Despite a strong showing by women, this alehouse, as my wife says, definitely has a "dude bar vibe," with sports on the two TVs flanking the bar, and man-chow like wings, nachos, burgers, and fries on their sturdy, pub-grub menu.

Mugs is what it is, and it's excellent at being just that: the OG craft beer bar in a neighborhood that's gone from working class to artists to hipsters to a tourist destination filled with Airbnbs, fancy-pants hotels, and millionaire condos. What Mugs is *not* is what Berestecki calls a "fantasy beer bar," referring to the latest wave of sleek, neon-free, ultrasophisticated craft beer tasting rooms. "Not everybody wants that," Berestecki says. "But they like a Weihenstephaner or a Hoegaarden. It's hard to keep up with the beer world now. I've given up even counting the new breweries opening up in New York anymore. It's gotten chaotic." At Mugs you'll get some of the best new brews, along with stalwarts like Smuttynose IPA, Anchor Liberty ale, Sierra Nevada pale ale, and, from the neighborhood brewery that kicked New York City craft brewing into gear, Brooklyn Brewery's flagship lager, which Berestecki has had on tap since October 1992.

MUGS *is* KNOWN FOR A COUPLE OF ANNUAL BEER EVENTS, AND IF YOU'RE INTO THE CRAFT BEER SCENE, YOU MIGHT WANT TO CHECK ONE OUT. <u>THE</u> BIGGIE *is the* UNNERVINGLY NAMED SPLIT THY BROOKLYN SKULL, A TWO-DAY WEEKEND FESTIVAL <u>IN</u> MARCH FEATURING A LINEUP *of* UNUSUAL, RARE, AND VERY, VERY STRONG BEERS (8 PERCENT ALCOHOL CONTENT AND ABOVE) FROM ACROSS THE COUNTRY *and* AROUND THE WORLD.

IN THE wee, drunk hours OF THE morning, a regular came in AND wanted his usual Coors Light. Berestecki told him he'd dropped Coors for Matt's Light, and, as Berestecki tells it, "The guy went totally bananas! He picked up a chair AND tried to bash me in the head."

WHEN TO GO

Saturday afternoons, when Mugs is pleasantly bubbly with a mix of locals who love it and beer geeks on pilgrimages from all over. Stick around, have some eats, and see the place really get going at night. Or, another excellent option, stop by Mugs for one of its special beer-tasting events; you'll find details in the events section of their website.

Happy hour: Monday to Friday, 2 to 7 p.m. $1 off all pints (except casks), house wine, and well drinks.

WHERE TO SIT

Grab a table in the elevated "mezzanine" section, to your right as you walk in the front door. Mugs is an ideal place to hang out with friends, drink beer, and talk, and that's best done at a table, especially if there are more than two of you. On warm afternoons, try to score one on the patio out back, get your pints, and while the day away.

WHAT TO DRINK

Start with a Smuttynose IPA. It's a fan favorite at Mugs, and they blow through gallons and gallons of it, so you're sure to get a fresh pint of very good beer from Hampton, New Hampshire. Then get whatever they have on tap from Brooklyn's own Other Half Brewing. "Their beers are phenomenal," says Berestecki. They brew about five miles from Mugs, so you'll get to enjoy a fresh IPA. And "a fresh IPA," as Berestecki says, "*is a thing of beauty*."

HOW TO GET THERE

Subway: The L train stops at Bedford Avenue, just three blocks from Mugs.

True story: Back in 1992, in the spot where Mugs now lives, Berestecki took over the Blue Rose and renamed the place Brooklyn Nights. It was a pretty standard corner bar with *very* standard beers on tap. One day Berestecki jazzed things up by taking Coors Light down and replacing it with Matt's Light, a perfectly accessible light beer from a brewer in Utica, New York. In the wee, drunk hours of the morning, a regular came in and wanted his usual Coors Light. Berestecki told him he'd dropped Coors for the new beer, and, as Berestecki tells it, "The guy went totally bananas! He picked up a chair and tried to bash me in the head. I wrestled it out of his hands, and after that I decided to take all the crap on tap off." He got rid of all the macrobrews, made the switch to only craft beers, and changed the name to Mugs, a name that came to Berestecki's wife, Halina, as she scanned the perimeter of the room, which was, and still is, loaded with mugs and steins from all over the world.

Every January Mugs has a "blind IPA" contest, which works like this: Berestecki and one other person hook up twelve kegs of IPAs to the lines in the basement. Each leads up to generic black tap handles at the bar labeled with the numbers one to twelve. Only Berestecki and his assistant know which beer corresponds to each tap. Participants receive small glasses with which they try as many four-ounce tastes of the beers as they like. At the end, participants vote for their favorites and receive souvenir pint glasses full of that beer. Berestecki tallies the score, and the winning IPA is put on one of Mugs' taps for the next twelve months. "I'm a hop-head," says Berestecki. "I love IPAs, even some of the real hoppy ones, and people are just hoppin' the *hell* out of these beers now."

A corner tavern has existed at this address for well over one hundred years, with the same bar the entire time, though that bar has *moved around* a bit. During Prohibition, the owner turned the front room into a "grocery store" and moved that big mahogany bar into the back, where the dining room is now located. Years later, the place was known as the Blue Rose, a bar owned by a Puerto Rican guy, where Berestecki used to hang out. On weekends, he recalls, the back room was a Polish disco, run by a friend of the bar's owner.

NEARY'S

358 East Fifty-seventh Street (at First Avenue)   MIDTOWN EAST, MANHATTAN
nearys.com   ·   *212-751-1434*

STEP INTO NEARY'S AND LEAVE THE COARSENESS OF NEW YORK CITY BEHIND. You're someplace special, warm, and civilized, a haven of lush abundance and good cheer. There's a dress code, gentlemen: collared shirts, please, and no jeans. I'd recommend clean shoes as well, to go with the elaborately patterned carpeting, paisley wallpaper, and all that gleaming wood and brass. This must be how it felt to go out before the sixties hit and decorum slipped more than a few notches.

You're surrounded by cushy elegance at Neary's: burgundies, browns, and gold, all quiet charm and relaxed hospitality. The music is low and soothing, the conversation civil and measured. You are always comfortable and well tended here. Your host Jimmy Neary and his staff—many of whom have been there for decades—make sure of it.

We first visited Neary's with another couple, forty-some years our senior and longtime regulars of the place. When we arrived, they were already settled into their favorite banquette seats, sipping their predinner cocktails. Neary himself greeted us warmly, with an "any friend of theirs is a friend of mine" graciousness.

We enjoyed an unhurried round of drinks before dinner, and our friend Al (north of ninety years old, great sense of humor) gestured toward the folks at the bar. "See that, John?" he said. "That's an *old-guy* pickup bar! All those guys in their seventies and eighties are working those *young women* in their sixties. Some of 'em will get 'em, too!" Sure, he was joking, but maybe only a little. Neary's has a lively, grown-up bar scene, anchored by its regulars (many of whom relocated after their venerable Upper East Side home base Elaine's closed in 2011) and a veteran team of bartenders, all fine hosts in their own right.

The tone of Neary's—warm charm and easy urbanity—is set by Neary himself, along with his daughter Una, a partner at Goldman Sachs, who works most weekends. A native of County Sligo, Ireland, Neary came to the United States in 1954 and worked in food service almost from the start. *Almost.* He was told on his first job interview, in a warehouse, that he was "too effin' small" for that gig. After a two-year stint in the U.S. Army and several jobs in food and bar service, in 1967 he and partner Brian Mulligan leased the ground floor of 358 East Fifty-seventh and turned a problematic location (three restaurants and two diners failed there in the six years preceding Neary's) into a tasteful New York institution. The vision was a stylish pub, more than a few steps up from shot-and-a-beer joints. "We put in the carpeting on the very first day," says Neary, "and always had a dress code." The rest, as they say, is history.

It's a classic place of "camaraderie and civility," says Neary, "with an atmosphere for conversation." Put on your good shoes, go with friends, and enjoy the old-Manhattan style and grace of this wonderful neighborhood pub.

Neary's has a lively, grown-up bar scene, anchored by its regulars (many OF whom relocated after their venerable Upper East Side home base Elaine's closed IN 2011) AND a veteran team OF bartenders, all fine hosts IN their own right.

WHEN TO GO	Any weekday at five, when people start coming in after work. I'd recommend a civilized cocktail hour at the bar followed by supper in the dining room.
WHERE TO SIT	The table in the far left corner of the dining room, where, as Jimmy says, "You can see the action at the bar and everybody in the whole place."
WHAT TO DRINK	Start with a classic martini. "Most people go with Beefeater," says bartender Tom Briody. "And Tito's is comin' on strong." They're big, cold, and dry as a bone, made with three to four ounces of liquor and "a tiny bit" of Tribuno vermouth. Don't miss the Irish coffee, great on its own or as dessert. It's made with care, and one of the best in town.
HOUSE RECIPE	**Neary's Irish Coffee**

About 2 ounces heavy cream
1½ ounces Power's Irish whiskey
1 tablespoon dark brown sugar
About 5 ounces hot coffee

Warm a sturdy stemmed glass by filling it with very hot water. Meanwhile, whip some heavy cream (Neary's uses a classic Hamilton Beach milkshake-style mixer) till it's a trifle thicker than house paint. Toss the hot water from the glass and add the whiskey, brown sugar, and coffee, leaving about an inch of room from the lip of the glass. Stir, then gently top with the cream by pouring it carefully over an inverted spoon, so the cool, white topping rests above the dark, hot liquid, looking not unlike a proper pour of Guinness stout.

Subway: The E and M trains stop at Lexington Avenue–53rd Street and the 4, 5, 6, N, R, and W trains stop at Lexington Avenue–59th Street, each about a ten-minute walk from Neary's.

WHAT ELSE?

Neary's is nestled among elite and powerful Manhattan neighborhoods like Sutton Place, the Upper East Side, and Midtown, its power location reflected in its clientele. Some call it "the Irish 21," a reference to another East Side eatery frequented by the rich and famous. Heavy hitters began coming in almost as soon as Neary's opened, including the congressman (later governor) Hugh Carey, New York governor George Pataki, and New York City mayor Michael Bloomberg. Check out the walls for a collection of signed photos, including those of Carey, Bloomberg, both presidents Bush, and Bill and Hillary Clinton, who spent New Year's Eve 2010 at Neary's on a triple date with Mayor Bloomberg and NYC Police Commissioner Ray Kelly.

MYSTERY WRITER AND REGULAR CUSTOMER MARY HIGGINS CLARK HAS INCLUDED JIMMY NEARY in OVER TWENTY of HER NOVELS SO FAR, and SEVERAL of HER BOOK COVERS ADORN THE PUB'S WALLS. "I DON'T READ THEM," NEARY ADMITS WITH A GRIN. "MARY JUST HIGHLIGHTS THE PARTS I'M IN and SENDS THEM to ME." IN CLARK'S BEST-SELLING LOVES MUSIC, LOVES TO DANCE, NEARY EVEN SOLVES THE MURDER.

Engage With
the Engaging Locals

So you're visiting New York. Or maybe you live here and you're just checking out a different *part* of New York. Good for you. It's healthy to leave your comfort zone and see what's out there.

Samuel Clemens once wrote, "Travel is fatal to prejudice, bigotry, and narrow-mindedness, and many of our people need it sorely on these accounts. Broad, wholesome, charitable views of men and things cannot be acquired by vegetating in one little corner of the earth all one's lifetime." Right on, Sam. You get out there, to a different country, a different state, even just a different city or neighborhood, and boom: your world expands. Your world*view* expands. *You* become bigger.

Part of that comes from just seeing where and how other people live, and part comes from actually *interacting* with them. When you do that, and get to know The Other, your "prejudice, bigotry and narrow-mindedness" dissolve, and in New York, loaded with Others, opportunities for such interaction abound.

You've probably heard these rumors about how rude New Yorkers are. Well, I'm here to tell you, that's a bunch of bull. New Yorkers can be vocal, direct, and unabashed in public, especially compared

to folks from the rest of the country. (I say this as someone who lived most of his life in Michigan before moving here in 2006.) That comes from living with nine million other people in one frenetic city. On occasion, there are moments, when you live in a densely populated pedestrian city, that call for . . . *frankness*, and sudden, necessary, unvarnished *communication*. It's merely expeditious. And *that*, to some people from outside of New York, can seem coarse. Abrupt. Rude, even.

My point is that New Yorkers aren't so much rude as vocally explicit, and there's a significant upside to that. In public spaces—bars and taverns, say—New Yorkers can be remarkably fun and easy to talk to, especially after you've had a glass or two of ye olde social lubricant. New Yorkers, especially on their home turf in their local bars, can be some of the most open, interesting strangers you will ever hang with: candid, quick, witty, and garrulous. Who better for a conversation?

When you're at a bar in New York, *especially* during a drinky, chatty time like happy hour, get involved in conversation. You may enjoy it, even if—maybe *especially* if—you end up listening to a kook prattle on for twenty minutes while you glaze over and smile. I've gotten in*to* or listened in *on* so many bar conversations while working on this book, covering topics like presidential trivia, beer, beer, more beer, the over-breeding of dogs, weird cat behavior, hidden history, food (the food you just ate, the food you *are* eating, the food you're *going* to eat after you *finish* the food you're eating now), cannibalism (ick), real estate drama (worse than cannibalism), the domino theory of state weed legalization, constructive use of psychedelic drugs, Hunter S. Thompson, art and madness, New Orleans Jazz Fest vs. Mardi Gras, the book of Genesis, the *band* Genesis, penile fracturing (shudder), travel anxiety, that guy's *deal*, the 2016 U.S. presidential election (the longest 287 months of my entire life), living overseas, the benefits and pitfalls of alcohol use, those fries and the likelihood of your *usin' 'em*, the adoption and (no joke) training of kittens, the splendor of middle age/prime of life, the Jungian concept of synchronicity, the Police's last album (Whoa! See? *Right there!*), love, health, the keys to a successful marriage, her *problem* and *what it might be*, *The Big Lebowski* as a metaphor for American political discourse during the Clinton years, *It's a Wonderful Life*, George Clooney's wonderful career, *The Venture Brothers*, the Smothers Brothers, Philip K. Dick–level conspiracy theories, the Yankees (suck/rule—discuss), the Mets (same), Tim Tebow, Wayne Thiebaud, cake vs. pie, Steely Dan: How could you hate?; the sociopolitical themes of *Battlestar Galactica*, Why Are We Here?, drivel, nonsense, pure and utter malarkey, the humane trapping of vermin, where to go next, and the weather, to name a few.

Take your cues from the crowd, the regulars and the bartender, and if the vibe seems right, chat it up. Maybe it starts with what someone's drinking or eating (New Yorkers can fetishize food, waxing about hamburgers like Keats did urns; see previous paragraph), the game that's on, or just the weather. Hey, that old chestnut still works for a reason. It's a nonconfrontational gateway topic.

According to linguist/philosopher Noam Chomsky, talking to people is one of the things we're hardwired to do. It's good for us, this interaction with others, as Samuel Clemens pointed out, too. In New York, especially at a "talkin' bar," you can find as much conversation as you want. Sometimes *more*, but hey, that's a chance you take.

NEIR'S TAVERN

87-48 Seventy-eighth Street (at Eighty-eighth Avenue)   WOODHAVEN, QUEENS
neirstavern.com · 718-296-0600

NEIR'S TAVERN FEELS KIND OF LIKE AN OLD LIBRARY, only with lots of exceptionally cold beer and hot pub food—the kind of library Homer Simpson would gladly spend some time in. A *libeery*. Old wood flanks you when you walk into this corner spot, the original mahogany bar on your right, a set of windowed cabinets to your left, showing their age, listing slightly to the right—along with the wooden building itself—over the course of several decades.

Owner Loy Gordon pins the opening of the bar to 1829, when Cadwallader Colden opened the Blue Pump Room in this spot, at that time a tavern conveniently located directly across from the main entrance to the enormous Union Course, where seventy thousand fans could watch the greatest sporting spectacle of the day: horse racing. The track was made of dirt, not grass, a game-changing innovation of the time, and for decades some of the biggest races in the country were held right there, surrounded by farmland and a few houses. The big North-South race took place at the Union Course for years, with champion horses from the South and the North facing off in a spectacle of national prominence that brought people from all over the States to little old Woodville (as it was then known). Colden nailed the first rule of business: location.

By the eighteen sixties the track closed and things quieted down. All that racetrack land was sold to developers, and the old tavern found itself across the street from a bunch of modest two-story homes, on a quiet intersection a few blocks from the train that eventually became the Long Island Rail Road. Known as the Old Abbey then, it sold Joseph Eppig's made-in-Brooklyn beer. In 1898 Louis Neir bought the place and gave it his name.

Woodhaven grew and changed over the years, but Neir's remained, serving the locals till it nearly went under in 2009. "It almost became a bodega," Gordon says. "But I said, 'That's not happening. We're doing something.'" Gordon, a New York City Fire Department lieutenant with zero experience in the food-and-beverage business, pooled his money with other investors and bought the place in the nick of time. He wants Neir's to stay around for another century or two, so he's working to get it designated as a historic landmark with help from fact-diggers like Richard Hourahan of the Queens Historical Society and Ed Wendell, president of the Woodhaven Cultural and Historical Society.

So, yes, it's a place of local history (and those local *historians*, who hang out there), with a strong claim to the much-contested title of Oldest Bar in New York City. But at its heart, Neir's is an accessible,

friendly corner bar, the clientele as unfussy and diverse as its home borough of Queens. Sure, they might be hanging out in the oldest bar in town, but it's just their neighborhood joint, a comfortable, reliable place to meet friends for dinner, watch a ball game, or hold a birthday party in the back room. There's definitely a little bit of Cheers in Neir's. "I wanted to be like Sam Malone," bartender Marie Rizzo told me, referring to the boss of that legendary TV bar. "That's why I became a bartender!"

Neir's spans generations. Gordon told me that a guy in his early thirties came into Neir's one day, sat at the end of the bar, ordered a beer, and thanked Gordon for saving the place. Gordon answered, of course, that it was his pleasure. The guy continued: "I don't know if you understand. I loved my father, and this was his favorite place. I didn't know him too well—he was a man's man—but now, here I am, in his favorite seat, and it feels like I'm having a beer with him."

"Neir's isn't a trendy place," Gordon says. "We don't get packed, generally speaking, but we want to last forever. When you come here, you're gonna get what's tried-and-true." Gordon, who moved from Jamaica (the island) to Jamaica (the neighborhood in Queens) when he was a little kid, was embraced by the mostly older, Irish crowd at Neir's as a young man with the FDNY. "When I came in here, people made me feel like I was one of them. And I looked *nothing* like them!"

Queens is regularly called one of the most ethnically diverse places in the world, with no single racial or ethnic group making up over half its population. The clientele at Neir's reflects this, too. "It's an American bar with American food. We serve all kinds of people from the neighborhood. This IS America."

AFTER LOUIS NEIR BOUGHT the PLACE IN 1898, HE SPRUCED IT UP, ADDING HOTEL ROOMS, A COUPLE of BOWLING LANES in the BASEMENT, AND EVEN A SMALL STAGE. RECHRISTENED AS NEIR'S SOCIAL HALL, IT WAS POPULAR FOR VAUDEVILLE-ERA SHOWS, INCLUDING SOME PERFORMANCES by the CURVACEOUS LOCAL LASS MARY JANE WEST, LATER KNOWN as MAE.

WHEN TO GO

Hit Neir's on a weekend afternoon, when you can usually get a seat at the old Honduran mahogany bar and hang out with some locals.

Happy hour: Monday to Friday, 4 to 7 p.m. $3 drafts, wine, well drinks, and select bottled beers.

WHERE TO SIT	The seat at the rightmost end of the bar, next to the window that faces Seventy-eighth Street. There you'll have a perfect view of the entire front room, most of the back, and the front door, so you can see who's coming and going.
WHAT TO DRINK	Go classic, and get a Bud or Guinness as cold as you'll ever have. The wondrous old-fashioned tap system at Neir's has twelve feet of coiled piping leading from each keg to its tap, all packed in fresh ice. Your beer will be deliciously frosty, even in the dead of August. Feeling saucy? Order a Mae West Punch, named for the bombshell who used to perform on the stage at Neir's long ago. Never had a Mae West Punch before? Try it. As the lady herself said, "When caught between two evils, I generally pick the one I've never tried before."

Neir's Mae West Punch

1 ounce vodka
1 ounce white rum
1 ounce gin
½ ounce grenadine
1½ ounces Red Bull energy drink

Combine the vodka, rum, gin, and grenadine in a cocktail shaker with ice. Shake well, strain into a large glass full of ice, and top with the Red Bull. Garnish with an orange wedge and a cherry and serve with a straw.

HOW TO GET THERE	Subway: The J and Z trains stop at 75th Street–Elderts Lane, a few blocks from Neir's.
WHAT ELSE?	Two of the great scenes from Martin Scorsese's *Goodfellas* were filmed at Neir's: "Bring It Back," where Jimmy Conway (played by Robert De Niro) throws a Christmas party to celebrate the wildly successful Lufthansa heist, only to find his cohorts have defied his instructions and tossed down their share of the money on ridiculously conspicuous things like cars, mink coats, and blondes; and the infamous "Shinebox" scene, where Joe Pesci and De Niro beat made man Billy Batts to a pulp after his incessant needling of Pesci's character, wiseguy Tommy DeVito—former shoeshine boy and full-time psycho.

OLD TOWN BAR

45 East Eighteenth Street (between Broadway and Park Avenue South)　UNION SQUARE, MANHATTAN
oldtownbar.com　·　*212-529-6732*

THE OLD TOWN IS A GORGEOUS, CLASSIC BAR with a very human vibe. You won't hear a TV when you walk in. They have one, but the volume is almost always low or completely off. You might not even hear music, usually also playing at or below indoor-voice level. What you *will* hear are the voices of actual, live *people*. People who come there, self-selected, to eat, drink, and talk.

It's a vocal bar, and New York through and through. "What really distinguishes us is that most of our employees are New York–born and –raised, with a connection to the city." So says owner Gerard Meagher, whose New York family roots date back to the early eighteen hundreds in Brooklyn. Soak up the old New York vibe of his place: dozens of photos of drinkers past, pennants and posters from Fordham (Meagher's alma mater), a signed headshot of Whitlow Wyatt, who pitched for the Brooklyn Dodgers from 1939 to 1944.

This bar's old (opened in 1892), as you can tell from the beveled mirrors, brass fixtures, pressed-tin ceiling, and all that deep, dark mahogany. A small brass plaque on the front of the fifty-five-foot-long marble-top bar confirms it was built by C. Rieger's Sons at 450-52 East 148th Street in the Bronx, an address long since converted to apartments.

The Old Town was once a German place called Viemeister's, then a speakeasy during Prohibition fortunate to have friends just around the corner at Tammany Hall. The neighborhood was once a Democratic workingman's haven, and Gerard Meagher's father Larry, a photo engraver with the *New York World-Telegram*, was one of them. The Old Town, near his union hall, became his regular bar.

After his stint in news, Larry Meagher got into the bar business, and by the seventies was working at the Old Town, eventually taking over for owners Henry and Bernice Lohden. In what was then a gritty, run-down, junkie-infested neighborhood, Larry saw an unpolished gem. He expanded the Old Town's hours of operation, reopened the kitchen, and brought the beautiful second-floor dining room back into service. Gerard became a bartender in the seventies and took over after his father died in 2007.

He's adamant about keeping the Old Town as it is: a classic New York tavern, defined primarily by its timeless charm, beauty, and character. "Too many bars are segmented—gay bar, working guy bar, hipster bar—but not here. We own the building, and we can keep prices low. We don't kowtow to celebrities, and we treat everyone with respect."

IF YOU DON'T REMEMBER *the* OPENING MONTAGE *for* LATE NIGHT WITH DAVID LETTERMAN FROM *the* LATE EIGHTIES, CHECK IT OUT ONLINE. THE CAMERA SWOOPS RIGHT INTO *and* THROUGH THE OLD TOWN AS PAUL SHAFFER AND THE WORLD'S MOST DANGEROUS BAND PLAY DAVE'S THEME, AND BILL WENDELL ANNOUNCES *the* NIGHT'S LINEUP.

WHEN TO GO	"Any afternoon during the week, when it's not too crowded, so you can get a good look at the beauty of the place," says Meagher.
WHERE TO SIT	Meagher likes "the catbird seat" at the end of the bar, against the wall to the left just as you walk in the door, where you can see the whole place. I personally prefer the first booth on your right as you walk in. I call it the Talkin' Booth, where you meet with friends for long, uninterrupted conversations.
WHAT TO DRINK	In summer, get a lemonade and vodka, a quencher they make with fresh-squeezed lemons. In colder weather, have a hot cider with brandy, whiskey, or rum. In autumn, Gerard's sister buys the cider fresh in upstate New York and delivers it to the bar every week.
HOW TO GET THERE	Subway: The 4, 5, 6, L, N, R, Q, and W trains all stop at Union Square, just a block south.

And, in the name of glory, I can't fail to mention those Porcelain Wonders of the World, Old Town's mighty Hinsdale urinals. A gala celebration marked their centennial in 2010, and you'll see a framed poster commemorating the event (made by the granddaddy of the letterpress process, Hatch Show Prints of Nashville, Tennessee) hanging to the left of the men's room door. These urinals . . . they're enormous. Positively Bunyanesque. They're the RMS *Queen Marys* of lavatory fixtures. Small boys would be wise to heed their gravitational pull. I'm just saying they're pretty big urinals, is all.

"ONE DAY SEAMUS HEANEY CAME IN *with* BRYAN FRIEL. WE HAD THE BEST LIVING IRISH POET *AND* PLAYWRIGHT RIGHT HERE IN ONE PLACE," RECALLS MEAGHER. LOOK *on the* WALL TO YOUR LEFT AS YOU WALK IN, THERE BY THE CATBIRD SEAT. YOU'LL SEE A SIGNED COPY *of THE REDRESS OF POETRY* BY HEANEY, RIGHT BELOW FRANK McCOURT'S *ANGELA'S ASHES and* THOMAS KELLY'S *PAYBACK*.

PETE'S TAVERN

129 East Eighteenth Street (at Irving Place)   GRAMERCY PARK, MANHATTAN
petestavern.com · *212-473-7676*

NEW YORK'S GOT A LOT OF "OLDEST BARS." Records are patchy, legends get repeated as history, and the definition of "oldest"—and "bar," for that matter—is debatable. But Pete's Tavern is one of them. Since 1864 they've continuously served beer, whiskey, and wine at the corner of Irving Place and East Eighteenth, right through Prohibition, the blackouts of 1977 and 2003, and during both Hurricanes Irene and Sandy. That's an indisputably solid run, plus Pete's had one of the best Prohibition scams I've ever heard.

Like many taverns of its founding era, the place is divided into a front barroom (with an entrance on Irving Place) and a back dining room (with an entrance on East Eighteenth Street), connected by a portal. During Prohibition, they swapped out their tavern sign for one that said FLORIST, and backed it up by filling the barroom's windows with flowers and heavy curtains. The front entrance was permanently closed, leaving the side door, on Eighteenth Street, as the "florist's" only functional entry. If you walked in off the street, you'd see what appeared to be a modest flower shop, with a counter in front and a large, walk-in refrigerator full of fresh posies to your left. That "refrigerator" had a hidden back door, though, which led through the connecting portal into the barroom, fully operational throughout America's so-called Noble Experiment. The party went on at Pete's for thirteen years without a hitch, customers coming and going through that magic refrigerator. Look for the photos of Pete's in its flower-shop days up on the walls today.

Pete's is a historic gem, and (minus the framed photos of more contemporary celebrities) looks like it could exist comfortably in 1963, 1933, or even 1883. "It's the charm, honestly," is what general manager Gary Egan says he loves about the place where he's worked since he arrived from Dublin in 1987, "and the fact that it's never changed." And it can't change *too* much, either. Number 129 East Eighteenth Street is a landmarked building, which means it's a real pain in the ass to make even minor alterations to the exterior. Signage, windows, painting, anything like that has to be approved by the Landmarks Preservation Commission, a *good* bureaucracy, if you ask me, but a bureaucracy nonetheless, and one reason Pete's is so wonderful. Go in and feel the history, especially during lunch or the midafternoon, when you can take your time and soak up the tavern's beauty.

The majestic rosewood bar was probably installed around nineteen hundred by New York's largest brewer, George Ehret, who owned the marvelously named Hell Gate Brewery on Manhattan's Upper East Side. Pete's (then called Healy's Café) was one of dozens of taverns Ehret owned around the city,

all selling his beer exclusively. Brewery-owned bars were quite common before Prohibition, and their owners' deep pockets allowed for some gorgeous settings to showcase their beer. No exception, Pete's backbar is fully decked out with beveled glass and mirrors, built-in light sconces, and even a grandfather clock. Now *that's* a bar. The bar is meticulously maintained, as is the entire place, consistently A-rated by the New York City Department of Health. "A *B* is the bane of a New York restaurant," says Egan. Diligent maintenance keeps Pete's clean as a whistle and gleaming like a Smithsonian treasure.

Example: In the entryway, you'll notice a couple of thick, curved, narrow (and *damned expensive-looking*) windows. Egan pointed out a brutal crack in one, the recent result, he guessed, of a carelessly swung backpack with a laptop in it or a very, *very* sharp elbow. "This here? This'll cost about fifty-two hundred dollars to replace," he told me. That's a lot of pints. After a low whistle, I asked if he intended to commit to such a spendy repair. He looked me dead in the eye and said, "Oh, yes, of course. We *have* to."

Pete's IS A *historic gem,* AND *(minus the framed photos of more contemporary celebrities) looks like it could exist comfortably* IN *1963, 1933,* OR *even 1883.*

WHEN TO GO	After work on weekdays. Catch the full wave of happy hour revelry at the gorgeous old bar, then stick around for dinner in one of the booths. *Happy hour: Monday to Friday, 4 to 7 p.m. Complimentary hors d'oeuvres and $5 pours of select beer and wine.*
WHERE TO SIT	Booth three (which is to the right as you walk in), where O. Henry is reputed to have written his beloved short story, "Gift of the Magi." You get all the atmosphere of the barroom there, while tucked away from the crowd in your own little nook.
WHAT TO DRINK	Start out with the house beer: Pete's 1864 ale, a slightly sweet amber made exclusively for Pete's by Matt Brewing of Utica, New York. End with a coffee drink. I've rarely if ever seen so many on one menu. There are *eight*, and they're perfect after a meal. I recommend Pete's Coffee Royale, made with brandy and a trio of liqueurs. It's a dessert and a pick-me-up at the same time.

PETE'S TAVERN

Pete's Coffee Royale

½ ounce Kahlúa
½ ounce Nuyens French brandy
½ ounce Frangelico
½ ounce Grand Marnier
1 ounce half-and-half
About 5 ounces hot coffee
Whipped cream

Put the Kahlúa, brandy, Frangelico, Grand Marnier, and half-and-half in a prewarmed Irish coffee mug. Fill with hot coffee to within an inch of the cup's lip. Top with a hefty dollop of whipped cream.

Subway: The 4, 5, 6, L, N, Q, and R trains all stop at 14th Street–Union Square, just three blocks away.

Check out all the celebrity photos on the walls, which—yes, I know—are sort of corny, but undeniably a blast. "People go crazy for 'em," says Egan. Come on: Tell me it's not kind of a thrill to see Patti Smith hanging out right where you are. Or Mickey Mantle, Brad and Angie, James Cagney, Walter Cronkite, Anne Hathaway, Bill Murray, two Sutherlands (a young Donald and an older Kiefer), Toms Selleck *and* Hanks, several vintages of Johnny Depp, and even—for Pete's sake—*Patty freakin' Duke.* How about Bernadette Peters and Mandy Patinkin on a date? A bunch of World Champ '69 Mets blowing the suds off their beers? Ricky Gervais, Ronnie Spector, Telly Savalas, Willie Nelson! They're fun, and these photos complement Pete's physical history with cultural—let's say *pop* cultural—history.

Getting engaged? Do it at Pete's. "We had a guy come in once," Egan says. "He proposed to his girlfriend here, and said he was the third generation to do that at Pete's, along with his father and grandfather. Said he hopes we'll still be here for his son's engagement, and make it four generations running. I said we will." The place has an undeniable romantic pedigree. (Hey, even *Sex and the City*'s Miranda popped the question to her guy Steve as they drank beer at the sidewalk café here.) What's more, Egan told me that eight of the past ten general managers (himself included) met their spouses at Pete's.

THE POUR HOUSE OF BAY RIDGE

7901 Third Avenue (at Seventy-ninth Street)   BAY RIDGE, BROOKLYN
pourhousebayridge.com   ·   718-491-6658

I DON'T REMEMBER WHO TOLD ME to check out the Pour House of Bay Ridge, but I'm glad they did. It's in a part of town I'd only visited once, and being a neophile—someone who appreciates novelty—I like that. Separated from the rest of Brooklyn by the Gowanus Expressway and the Belt Parkway, and served by only one subway line, Bay Ridge has a localness to it that you don't often find in New York City, and that's reflected in its bars, too.

The Pour House sits at the corner of Seventy-ninth Street and Third Avenue, one of the main commercial drags in Bay Ridge. It's a spare, open, straightforward corner sports bar with good pours and fair prices, anchored by loyal neighborhood regulars—mostly guys watching the games on weekend afternoons, a younger mixed crowd at night. It's a place to meet your pals, unwind after work, rev up for a Friday evening out, or just watch sports, drink beer, and break your friends' balls.

It's a hyper-local place, but on a July Sunday we were welcomed right away, with top-notch, friendly service by Chris Byrne, one of the bar's three partners and, in his early thirties, the youngest. The forty-something guys from the Pour House softball team at the end of the bar razzed each other (and Byrne) with tough-guy good nature, and fed the jukebox the whole time. (I love when people feed the jukebox. It's generous and seems to happen a lot at locals bars.)

The large windows facing Third Avenue are often open, so the clean ocean breeze blows right in past the Verrazano-Narrows Bridge (which you can see a few blocks to the south), filling the place with fresh air. Bay Ridge, historically a strong, middle-class community of Irish, Italians, and Greeks, is now home to a number of Lebanese, Russians, Poles, Chinese, and Hispanics as well. You'll see all these cultures, and more, represented in the businesses on Bay Ridge's wide avenues. Byrne calls the Pour House "a workingman's bar," and it's a cop/fireman/municipal worker/schoolteacher kind of place. No frills, plenty of TVs, and a hell of a good host. Byrne, a workingman for sure, grew up a couple of blocks away and went from barback to partner in seven years. He covers a lot of shifts behind the stick and was born to play the role of barman.

"I love *this*," he said, gesturing at the crowd on a football Sunday. "I love meeting new people. I love hanging out with people and showing 'em a good time." This is a case when the bartender *makes* the bar, setting it above the rest.

166

_**THE** large windows facing Third Avenue are often open,
so the clean ocean breeze blows right in past the Verrazano-Narrows Bridge
(which you can see a few blocks to the south), filling the place with fresh air._

On our first visit, my wife sized the place up, looking at the menus and glancing around the bar, and noticed the Pour House's impressive whiskey list. Byrne appreciated her interest and insisted she try one of his favorites, which he admitted was expensive as he poured her a free sample. Around this same time, some regulars were getting feisty in their storytelling and she glanced in their direction—which one of them worried might be a look of offense, as apparently they'd been using what a lady might consider off-color language. She shook her head and said no, she wasn't offended and hadn't heard anything anyway, but one of the fellas wanted to make amends, so he pointed to her glass and said, "Chris, what's she drinking?" Without missing a beat, Byrne smirked and said she was drinking the high-priced whiskey and served up a hefty pour, sticking the guy with a hefty bill. The regular, "Toes," obliged like a gent. Expert hosting, all around, with good-natured, ball-busting, old-Brooklyn style.

Bay Ridge is a paradise of local businesses, the kind that disappear when neighborhood rents get too high, their leases lost to corporate giants with deep pockets like big banks, fast-food joints, and retail chains. When a local tavern in our neighborhood met that sad fate recently, flipping from longtime corner bar to chic clothing store, our neighbor Geoff lamented, "What did our neighborhood ever do to deserve a *rag & bone*?"

Whatever it was, it hasn't happened—*yet*—in Bay Ridge.

WHEN TO **GO**

On a Sunday afternoon to watch a game. Football, baseball, hockey, hoops, curling, whatever's in season. Byrne will likely be behind the bar, and you'll have a good time. "It's not even like working," he told me one Sunday, with the Giants/Browns game on the TV behind him. "It's like hanging out with friends."

Happy hours: Daily, noon to 7 p.m.: $1 off "just about everything." Special happy hour for teachers every Friday, 3 to 7 p.m.: $2 Bud Light drafts. (And really, don't they deserve it?)

WHERE TO **SIT**

At the end of the bar by the front windows, next to the wooden cigar-store Indian called Patrick. (He's good luck.) The Pour House is a *bar* bar, with almost no place to sit *except* at the bar, and that's where you want to be. Byrne guarantees that "your service will be good. The *best*."

You can't go wrong with a cold draft beer and/or a neat pour of craft whiskey. They have ten taps to choose from and over a dozen whiskeys, a list that changes every two months.Or boldly order the damnedest cocktail I've had in a while, the Space Cowboy, made with vodka and Tang (yes, the orange breakfast drink of astronauts). It's like the official screwdriver of the Apollo program. Have one or two and they'll be calling you Buzzed Aldrin.

The Space Cowboy

A generous quantity of Absolut vodka
An equal quantity of premixed Tang and water

Freely pour both ingredients simultaneously into a large glass full of ice until brimming. (Consider it a sort of liquid space race.) Serve with a plastic straw. I commented to Byrne on the nice, big pour the bartender put into my Cowboy. He just beamed and said, "Welcome to the Pour House."

Subway: The R train stops at 77th Street, about four blocks away.

Like a lot of small neighborhood places, the Pour House doesn't serve food, but you're welcome to order delivery or pickup and chow down at the bar. And you're in Bay Ridge, a neighborhood filled with excellent, locally owned restaurants. The bartender will give you the menus they stash behind the bar, if you ask, and surely some suggestions. Bay Ridge is rich in small-scale family businesses and restaurants. Support them with your bucks.

Look around. Do you see that officious, ubiquitous "maximum occupancy" sign anywhere? No, you don't. "This corner has been a bar for about ninety years," Byrne told me with a big ol' beer-drinkin' grin. "There *is* no 'maximum occupancy.' It's grandfathered in."

RADEGAST HALL & BIERGARTEN

113 North Third Street (at Berry Street)   WILLIAMSBURG, BROOKLYN
radegasthall.com   ·   *718-963-3973*

WALK INTO RADEGAST HALL & BIERGARTEN, take in the spacious, woody barroom and its handsome red oak bar, then hang a sharp right and plant yourself in the biergarten. Usually I prefer sitting at a bar, but the biergarten—that's where the soul of this place is, with the big communal tables, the skylights they crank open on nice days, and the grill. Just as the kitchen is the "heart of a home," the grill room/beer hall is the heart of Radegast.

It's wide open in there, the ceiling peaking at over twenty feet above folks at tables on both sides of the long room. Their voices bounce all over the place. You smell something enticing and summery, and there at the end of the room you see the grillmeister flipping sausages and burgers, fan-pulled smoke brushing past his face.

Ah, this is good. Take a seat. Order a beer from one of the busy women clad in black and scarlet. Order a pretzel while you're at it. They're huge, the size of a steering wheel, speckled with coarse salt and served with fresh, spicy-sweet house mustard. Oh, and they're baked to order, so they come to you hot as the blazes of Hades and blessed with a sort of rigid, bagel-y outer shell and steaming, pillowy innards. Want beer cheese with that? Yes, you do, but this pretzel is so good, you don't really need it.

Radegast Hall & Biergarten opened in 2007, the vision of its Slovakian-born partners, Ivan Kohut and Andy Ivanov. They took over one of Williamsburg's brawny old factory/warehouse spaces and built it out with lots of reclaimed wood to give it that old-time, been-there-awhile feel. Ten years on, in a radically different, mega-gentrified Williamsburg, the place is still going strong. That's due in large part to solid fundamentals like location, decor, and a strong beer-and-food menu, but then there's the live music, which puts Radegast in a whole other league.

A Middle European beer hall with one of New York City's best daily jazz lineups. Who'da thunk? Jazz fans and Lindy Hoppers from all over show up to catch acts like Baby Soda, the Sugartone Brass Band, Emily Asher's Garden Party, New Orleans's fabulous Meschiya Lake, and gypsy jazz guitar virtuoso Stephane Wrembel. There's a lot of love at Radegast. A lot of love and a lot of fun.

RADEGAST GRILLS UP SOME MEAN SAUSAGES, *and* THEY'RE
MADE FRESH *by* FAMILY PRODUCERS WHO'VE BEEN DOING IT
LOCALLY *for* GENERATIONS. THEY ARE THE REAL DEAL,
AND THE SAUERKRAUT AND FRIES THAT COME WITH THEM
AIN'T BAD EITHER. (VEGETARIANS, EVEN THE PORTOBELLO
MUSHROOM SANDWICH IS GRILLED *with* TLC.)

RADEGAST HALL & BIERGARTEN

WHEN TO GO	Saturday or Sunday afternoon, when Radegast hosts live music with no cover in the beer hall. It's a hell of a good party, brimming with that rowdy, friendly, all-are-welcome beer-hall vibe. Want a nighttime scene? Stop in on a Wednesday or Thursday, when they run a special from four to close: buy a liter of any beer and receive a bratwurst on the house, hot off the grill. And as always, there's live music those nights, too, generally starting at nine.
WHERE TO SIT	Any seat in the beer hall, at one of the long, communal tables, where you and your comrades can almost always find a spot, especially if you're willing to squeeze in with a bunch of good-natured strangers, who will be even *better*-natured if you share your pitcher of Kölsch with them.
WHAT TO DRINK	You've really got to go with a beer here. Their most popular is the Hofbräu original, a refreshing lager brewed by one of Munich's oldest operations, in business since 1579. Does it pair well with steering-wheel-size, hot, salty pretzels? *Jawohl.* Next drink, and I'm going to get radical here: *another beer.* With thirteen taps in the front bar, nine more in back, and over one hundred bottles, my guess is you'll find one you'll like, but here's a suggestion: the Köstritzer Schwarzbier, a badass-looking, easy-drinking "black lager" from the Köstritzer brewery in Bad Köstritz, Germany, founded in 1543. And you know who liked Köstritzer Schwarzbier? Why, none other than Johann Wolfgang von Goethe himself, arguably the greatest man of letters the German peoples ever produced. Yep, Goethe "sustained himself on black beer from Köstritz when he was unable to eat during a period of illness." See? *Beer is good for you.* Goethe knew. (Don't like beer? Don't worry. Radegast has a full bar, some good wine, and, in season, superb hot drinks like mulled wine.)
HOW TO GET THERE	Subway: The L train stops at Bedford Avenue, five blocks from Radegast.
WHAT ELSE?	Look up on the wall in the main barroom and you'll see a portrait of two men with magnificent mustaches. They are Wilhelm II, emperor of Germany/king of Prussia, and his elderly buddy Franz Josef I, emperor of Austria/king of Hungary. On the downside (and it's a big downside), they helped bring us World War I, but then again, they reigned over some mighty fine beer-producing regions. *Prost,* fellas!

RADEGAST HALL & BIERGARTEN

Ballast

Exploring new bars in New York's wonderful neighborhoods is a blast. So is unwinding after work with colleagues at the local pub, or frittering away an entire Saturday afternoon with family and friends at a sun-dappled beer garden in July. But. *But* . . .

Alcohol is a toxin, my friends, and can extract a steep price: the wrath of the booze gods, brought down upon you brutally, like Thor's mighty hammer itself. This book is about the joy of social tippling, not getting spring-break wasted, so be smart and keep it fun. One of the best and most enjoyable precautions is food, or as some of my favorite booze writers call it, *ballast*. Good old starch and fat, the saltier the better. Something in the tank to soak up that ethanol and give the body some fuel and electrolytes to work with. It's a sound idea to eat before, during, and especially after drinking.

HELPFUL TIPS FOR MAINTAINING BALLAST

• **Eat before you go out.** Simple, huh? Apparently not. *(Damn our past mistakes!)* Eat first, because as you're drinking, judgment takes a nosedive and you're less likely to make good choices, like, say, eating. So keep it simple: chow down *before* going out. You'll have a better time and will thank yourself later.

• **Early in a drinking session, order some salty, starchy, and/or fatty snacks.** Right off the bat, and for the whole table. Cocktail peanuts, mozzarella sticks, crostini, bruschetta, an oil-cured Mediterranean olive medley. Orange popcorn, the fancy *salumi* platter, fried cheese curds, Zapp's Spicy Cajun Crawtator™ potato chips, delightful little toast points with the crusts cut off and tastefully appointed with delicate whispers of Marin County's finest organic *chèvre bleu*, I don't care. EAT. SOMETHING. That can be half the fun of a neighborhood bar: the eats! (Drink water, too, for that matter. A glass per round is a capital idea.)

• And *after* visiting a New York bar or two, I recommend a salty, greasy, piping hot slice of NYC pizza. It's about the cost of a subway ride and may be your last, best chance to avoid a profoundly unpleasant tomorrow. I know. *I've been there.* The Yelp app is especially helpful here, with all the info you need, excellent search/map interface to get you there, and enticing, foodporny Yelper photos.

RED LANTERN BICYCLES

345 Myrtle Avenue (between Carlton and Adelphi Streets)   FORT GREENE, BROOKLYN
redlanternbicycles.com   ·   347-889-5338

ON A BEAUTIFUL SUMMER DAY in Fort Greene, Brooklyn, I had grand ambitions to bike on up to Greenpoint, about as far north as you can go in this borough before hitting Queens. La Wiferina and I stopped for lunch first, and after the meal, I found my tire was flat. *Bummer*. The good news? Red Lantern was just a few blocks north.

I rolled my bike on in, past the folks eating brunch at the tables in front, past the bar on the right, and all the way to the bike shop in back, where I explained my situation to Sam Littlefield, the big, bearded dude working the counter. He said he'd fix it on the spot and suggested we wait at the bar and have a coffee, beer, or snack in the meantime.

Which we did. All was delicious (including fresh-baked goodies from Brooklyn's Northside Bakery and some tasty vegan options) and friendly. Meanwhile, Sam not only fixed the flat, he did it without my special wheel key, the kind you need so that no one can remove your wheels except you. Sam, a MacGyver of bike mechanics, figured out a way to get the job done fast, without the security key, and we were good to go.

Red Lantern is three important things to this vibrant Brooklyn neighborhood: coffee shop, bar, and bike shop. Three perfectly complementary elements in owner Brian Gluck's vision. "They all go together," he explains. "Like you see in the old black-and-white pictures of bikers in the Pyrenees, downing a beer during a ride, or an espresso before." He's right, it works; and as he said when he opened in 2011, Red Lantern was the first bike shop/café on the East Coast. A stream of people pass through, some rolling bikes to the back, others grabbing a cup of house-roasted coffee to go, while others park it at the bar for a cold beer and a bite.

When I told him about my fixed flat and the above-and-beyond service, Gluck wasn't surprised. "That sounds like Sam," he said. "Our mechanics are open, friendly, and accessible. They come around the counter to help you." Some bike shops can feel aloof. Not this one, and that tone is set by the man at the top. Gluck is a community *mensch*, a real good guy, and his shop is loaded with heart.

Gluck loves Fort Greene, and Fort Greene loves him and Red Lantern, too. Jerry Pura, a sociologist who lives nearby, confided, "Although he'd never tell you this, Brian helps neighborhood kids with no money fix their bikes, patch their tires and stuff." He also helps with various community events and fund-raisers. Gluck says, "If you have a bike-related event or a ride-based fund-raiser you want to hold here, we'll say yes ninety-nine percent of the time."

THERE'S A STRIKING MURAL *on the* WALL TO THE LEFT AS YOU WALK IN:
A REDHEADED BIKE GODDESS WHO LOOKS LIKE *an* ART NOUVEAU
DRAWING *by* ALPHONSE MUCHA, HOLDING A RED LANTERN *in*
FRONT OF HER TO ILLUMINATE THE WAY AS SHE SEEKS THE TRUTH . . .
OR MAYBE A GOOD LOCAL BEER *or* CREAMY NUT-MILK LATTE.
ARTIST LAURA MENSINGA PAINTED HER IN EXCHANGE *for* A LOCK,
HELMET, BIKE LIGHTS, *and* AN OVERHAUL.

Red Lantern is a community hub in Fort Greene, a place where all kinds of people cross paths and rub elbows. And this sort of casual interaction with the Other is healthy in a changing neighborhood as diverse as this one. It cultivates a chill, easy familiarity among neighbors, and breaks down the walls of class, age, and race. You'll see all types at Red Lantern: young, old, black, white, hip, square, overworked, underemployed, families, singles, couples, and friends. Everyone's there for bikes, beer, food, and coffee. It's a big tent, this place, and everyone's welcome.

PEOPLE POP *into* RED LANTERN *for* A LOT *of* DIFFERENT REASONS, *and* ONE IS TO VISIT *the* RESIDENT CELEBRITY, LAND SHARK THE SHOP CAT. HE'S A BIG, HANDSOME BEAST, OFTEN ASLEEP *on the* JOB, BUT, LIKE THE REST OF THE STAFF, ACCESSIBLE AND FRIENDLY.

WHEN TO GO

Gluck recommends daytime on Saturday or Sunday, when the place is in *high gear*, serving lots of food (not to mention bicyclers), and two baristas are working the bar. Another good bet is when there's a fund-raising event, and the community—whatever community that particular event might draw—shows up in force. And if you want to watch the Tour de France, this is the place.

Happy hour: Monday to Friday, 4 to 7 p.m., and weekends, 2 to 5 p.m. $1 off pints of draft beer and $3 bottles of Pabst Blue Ribbon.

WHERE TO SIT

The table by the window to the left as you walk in, for great sidewalk people-watching and sunshine.

WHAT TO DRINK

A cashew milk spiced chai latte, beloved by both vegans and dairy drinkers. Later in the day, how about a "hyper-local beer," as Gluck calls them? They always have a fine little selection of four or five New York brews (and often a cider) on tap, from operations like Sixpoint, KelSo, Rockaway Brewing, Braven, and SingleCut.

Cashew Milk

1 cup raw cashews
4 cups water
1 tablespoon honey or pure maple
  syrup
Pinch of salt

Soak the cashews in the water overnight in the refrigerator. Drain, reserving the soaking water, then rinse the nuts. Combine the cashews and half of the reserved water in a blender pitcher and blend until smooth (about 2 minutes). Add the rest of the reserved water, the sweetener, and the salt and blend again. Strain through a fine-mesh strainer, cheesecloth, or a nut-milk bag, discarding the leftover pulp. Transfer the milk to a jar, screw on the lid, and store in the refrigerator for up to 3 days.

HOW TO GET THERE

Subway: The C train stops at Lafayette Avenue; the G train stops at Fulton Street. Both are about a twelve-minute walk away. Or ride your bike and roll it in for a tune-up while you hang out.

WHAT ELSE?

If you have a bike-related event, you can probably hold it at Red Lantern, and these are fun to check out. On our first visit, there was a documentary screening/fund-raiser for bike messenger health care. They also host hands-on basic bicycle maintenance classes, where you learn how to take care of your wheels and get your hands good and greasy in the process, plus the bar hosts movie and beer-and-bingo nights.

RUBY'S BAR & GRILL

1213 Riegelmann Boardwalk (at Ruby Jacobs Walk)   CONEY ISLAND, BROOKLYN
rubysbar.com   ·   *718-975-7829*

SOME BARS TAKE A WHILE TO GROW ON YOU. Others get you the first time. That was Ruby's for me. When I walked in with my wife and our friends Twyla and Dr. Madrid on a beautiful September afternoon, the front of the bar was completely opened up to the boardwalk and the ocean breeze. The place was busy, but not so full we couldn't all get seats at the long bar. First I noticed the dark, rich gleam of old wood everywhere, then that great, greasy carnival smell of onions, peppers, and sausages sizzling on the grill.

We ordered a round, settled in, and noticed the music from the well-stocked jukebox. "Wagon Wheel" by Old Crow Medicine Show, "Oh Marie" by Louis Prima, "Rock With You" by Michael Jackson. A couple of Sinatra's finest, a little country, a little rock 'n' roll. The guy who'd been feeding the juke let me pick out a couple tunes on his dime. Dude now lives up in the Bronx but grew up in Coney, and travels all the way down most weekends to hang out at Ruby's.

Ruby's is special, a bar perched at the city's edge that turns out to be defined by its loyal, geographically scattered regulars. The place has the vacation energy of a classic beach bar, a mix of tourists and locals, all in a good mood, having a fine time.

This eclectic bunch wouldn't haul all the way in from Queens, Manhattan, the Bronx, etc., if Ruby's weren't worth it, and the manager, Mike Sarrel, makes sure it is. Sarrel married Melody Jacobs, daughter of the late Ruby Jacobs, the bar's namesake, and became part of the family tradition. "I come to work and *this* is my office: *the beach!*" he says with a sweep of his arm toward the boardwalk and beyond. Deborah Olin, a longtime "irregular regular" (Sarrel's term) from Manhattan who was born in nearby Brighton Beach, said of Sarrel, "He's a good man. Loyal, hardworking. He makes you feel good when you're here. It's like comin' home."

On another visit I met Holly Lane, a regular at Ruby's for over thirty-five years. She lives in the East Village, but the bar is her beach headquarters. She knows all the deeply tanned oldsters who hang out at the tables in front, soaking up solar energy, and many of the folks promenading, arm in arm, along the boardwalk. This community—people who love the beach, the boardwalk, and one another—are part of the good energy that's been building at Ruby's for years.

The structure itself went up around 1900 and became a bar in 1934, making it the oldest continuously running bar on the boardwalk, according to Sarrel. Ruby Jacobs bought it from Mike Shaw in

YOU'VE GOT TO HAVE A BITE TO EAT WHEN YOU'RE AT RUBY'S, SO LET'S NOT EVEN ARGUE ABOUT THIS.
THE AROMA is OBSCENELY IRRESISTIBLE, SO JUST GO FOR IT. YOU'RE ONLY HUMAN.
TAKE THE PROFESSIONAL ADVICE of MIKE THE GRILL GUY and ORDER A HOT or SWEET SAUSAGE WITH
ONIONS, PEPPERS, AND A ROLL. AND AS LONG AS YOU'RE AT IT, GET SOME FRIES, TOO.

RUBY'S BAR & GRILL

1972, running it till he died in 2000, when Melody and Mike took over. He was a beloved guy, Ruby. He loved Coney and Coney loved him. There's a story of the burglar alarm going off in the early-morning hours, back in the days when Coney Island was still pretty rough. Ruby walked in to find a guy robbing the bar. When he asked the guy why he broke in and the guy said he had no job, Ruby said, "You're hired." The busted burglar worked at Ruby's for the next thirteen years. Good energy.

Ruby's is special, a bar perched AT THE city's edge that turns out to be defined by its loyal, geographically scattered regulars. The place has the vacation energy of a classic beach bar, a mix of tourists and locals, all in a good mood, having a fine time.

WHEN TO GO	Any warm day during the afternoon, when Ruby's front is wide open to the boardwalk, beach, and sea. On summertime Friday nights, stick around for fireworks.
WHERE TO SIT	A table out front, on the boardwalk, where you can relax and take in the clean breeze and all the sun you can handle. "Look out there at the ocean," as Ruby once said. "Smell the air and look at the whole tapestry of people. Coney Island is the elixir of life!"
WHAT TO DRINK	Start with the house beer, Ruby's Amber, a rich, red American ale. Next drink: a Pink Mermaid, of course. You're in Coney Island, home of roller coasters, carny games, hot dogs, freak shows, and that gigantic, fabulous costume extravaganza, the annual Mermaid Parade.
HOUSE RECIPE	**Pink Mermaid**

1½ ounces vodka
½ ounce triple sec
A splash each of sour mix, 7Up,
  and cranberry juice

Combine all the ingredients in a large plastic Solo cup loaded with ice. Stir with a plastic straw and serve.

Subway: The D, F, N, and Q trains all stop at Stillwell Avenue, the end of the line, about three blocks from Ruby's. Walk toward the smell of the ocean and the sounds of the midway.

The walls are covered with hundreds of photos, posters, and framed reproductions of old Coney Island postcards. On the far wall to the right, you'll notice some rusty old metal Coke and Pepsi signs. Mike and Melody found them down below when they were doing renovations a few years ago. They're left over from the days when each building on the boardwalk also housed businesses *below*, in their lower levels. Until the sixties, you couldn't just waltz off the beach in a bathing suit and up onto the boardwalk, let alone into a boardwalk-level restaurant or bar, but *under* the boardwalk was a different story. Those places were accessible: no shirt, no shoes, no problem. As Coney's economy declined in the postwar era, the sub-boardwalk businesses closed, homeless people took over, and eventually the world under the boardwalk was completely filled with sand and forgotten.

THE GLEAMING OLD WOOD OF THE BAR, THE WAINSCOTING, THE COUNTERS, THE THRESHOLD LEADING IN from the BOARDWALK, THE INVERTED "GANGPLANK" UP on the CEILING (THE ONLY PLACE AT CONEY WHERE YOU CAN STILL GO "UNDER THE BOARDWALK") — THEY'RE ALL from CONEY'S ORIGINAL 1923 BOARDWALK. THESE PLANKS WERE TORN UP AROUND 2010 DURING RENOVATION. "THE CITY DIDN'T WANT IT, SO WE GOT IT FOR FREE," SAYS SARREL. THAT'S GREAT WOOD, TOO: BRAZILIAN IPE (SAY "EE-PAY"), EXTREMELY TOUGH, DENSE, and RESISTANT to INSECTS and ROT.

THE RUSTY KNOT

425 West Street (at West Eleventh Street)   WEST VILLAGE, MANHATTAN
cargocollective.com/therustyknot   ·   *212-645-5668*

I WAS TRUDGING THROUGH THE VILLAGE one Sunday afternoon during a hot, humid summer, and not too happy about it at all. This was in the middle of a marathon of ninety-plus-degree days, the air thick and filthy, and at three in the afternoon—peak heat—I needed a break. The Rusty Knot was a ten- to fifteen-minute walk away, so I went for it. I headed west, then west, then still a little farther west, until I eventually hit (of all things) West Street, the end of the road, nothing wester except the Hudson River, next stop Jersey. Thar it was, on the corner of West and Eleventh.

You wouldn't look twice at the exterior of the Knot, because for one thing, it's inconspicuously tucked into the bottom of a newish blocky brick condo building, and also, you might be speeding by at fifty miles per hour on the West Side Highway, aka West Street. A pretty unlikely spot for a refuge, matey, but bear with me.

Inside, it's cool, easy on the eyes, and comfortable. All caramel-colored wood paneling and checkerboard flooring the colors of water and reeds. You're safe from the pounding sun, like a kid sitting under a willow tree "fort," its draping branches and leaves protecting you from the World Out There. With a hot, roaring highway a few feet away, you would not expect this, but here it is, an urban oasis.

I took a seat at the end of the modest bar, ordered a draft of Busch beer (rarely seen these days in NYC), a pretzel dog, and a bowl of house-made pickles, and settled in. The bartender Ryan, a total pro, set me up in a jiffy, then went on to his next task. I started looking at all the stuff on the walls, which is plenty, because the Knot has a certain theme, you know, and by law nautical bars must sport a minimum number of seafarin' things, or they're fined or something. Keel-hauled. Pretty soon I noticed, "Hey, all this stuff is actually pretty good!" Well chosen, clean, interesting, and, overall, tasteful, in a kitschy-chic way. The whole place was like that. There's intelligence behind this joint.

"It's like your uncle's lake house in the eighties," says Victor, the general manager. The Knot is a thrifter's dream of midcentury vacation-cottage furniture and artifacts, from artistic (surprisingly good garage-sale paintings) to goofy (the PLEASE BE NICE TO THE BARTENDER—HELP IS HARD TO GET PBR sign, circa 1970). Victor tells me, "This place is Ken's oasis." Owner Ken Friedman also owns the famed gastropub the Spotted Pig, just down Eleventh Street. His vision was to create an accessible, casual place in the far, *far* West Village, a part of town where that sort of thing hasn't existed for years, since the days of docking and shipping faded and millionaire condos sprouted up

I started looking AT *all the stuff on the walls, which is plenty, because* THE *Knot has a certain theme, you know,* AND *by law nautical bars must sport a minimum number* OF *seafarin' things,* OR *they're fined* OR *something. Keel-hauled.*

like mushrooms. The Rusty Knot is a high-concept, modern nod to the old riverfront bars that once lined the Hudson. Friedman wanted to create a low-key, tasteful "dive" where he could hang out after working at the Spotted Pig, and anybody from the neighborhood (and beyond) could come as they are. He did, and they *do*. "We get some people coming in after black-tie events and others after their run along the river."

On that hot day I first visited, I sipped my beer, enjoyed my tasty eats, listened to a surprisingly broad mix of jukebox tunes, and admired the striking painting on the backbar, featuring a view of the old Hudson waterfront circa 1947, flanked by two *woof*-tastic pinup girls from the era. Hunkered down in my cool, shady haven, my back to the West Side Highway, I felt miles away from the heat, noise, and dirt of the sweltering Manhattan summer beyond the door.

WHEN TO GO	For peace: weekday evenings at sunset. "There's a five- to ten-minute window when the view's amazing for anyone in the place," says Victor. For a *party*, stop by any Sunday from four to ten, when they throw a good old Fire Island–style tea dance. A tea dance, you ask? Look it up online.
	Happy hour: Monday to Friday, 4 to 7 p.m. Two-for-one well cocktails and Busch drafts. Plus happy hour specials all day Tuesdays.
WHERE TO SIT	The deck furniture near the big front windows, perfect for watching the sun set.
WHAT TO DRINK	When you're at the Rusty Knot, you *drink* a Rusty Knot: a frothy, frozen, minty daiquiri, a perfect "beach drink" for a warm summer day. Later, try a Pickle Back, a two-ounce shot of Jameson Irish whiskey immediately followed by a two-ounce shot of brine from the Rusty Knot's wonderful house-made pickles. (The brine's salty electrolytes are alleged to ward off hangovers.)

The Rusty Knot

2 ounces Flor de Caña 4-year-old
gold rum
1 ounce simple syrup (equal parts
sugar and water, stirred or
shaken until the sugar completely
dissolves)
5 dashes of Angostura bitters
8 to 10 mint leaves
1 heaping cup ice cubes

Combine all the ingredients in a blender and let 'er rip until you have a smooth and slushy mix. Pour into a highball glass and serve with a straw.

Subway: The 1 train stops at Christopher Street–Sheridan Square, about a ten-minute walk to the Knot.

Spend some time with that mural behind the bar, the one with the hubba-hubba girls. It's beautiful, a moody sunset scene from a time long-gone, with storm clouds brewing over the ship-filled Hudson, a view of the river from about where the Rusty Knot sits today. Friedman commissioned the piece from artist Robert Garey of Florence, South Carolina, who's a master of large-scale period pieces.

The Rusty Knot's jukebox is free. Oh, how I love that. "A bar without music is like whiskey without pickle brine," as my dear old mom never once said, and this juke, a classic, CD-stocked Rowe AMI Encore model, is chock-full of all kinds of tunes. Metal, hippie jams, grunge, seventies wimp-rock, new wave. Old country, outlaw country, soul, dance, punk. Patsy Cline, Willie Nelson, Tina Turner, Michael Jackson, Beck. The Clash, the Smiths, the Byrds, the Doobies, the B-52s, and the freakin' Pet Shop Boys! Lionel Richie, Nirvana, Rob Base and DJ E-Z Rock, Helmet, and Asia. *Asia, for the love of . . . !* All for free. Zip. Diddly. Bubkis. *Niente.* Enjoy your complimentary tunes with one of the city's cheapest pool tables: fifty cents per game, under an old Budweiser billiard chandelier.

SHRINE

2271 Adam Clayton Powell Jr. Boulevard (between West 133rd and West 134th Streets)   HARLEM, MANHATTAN
shrinenyc.com · *212-690-7807*

WALK IN AND THE FIRST THINGS YOU'LL NOTICE are the walls and ceiling. The room is a cool collage of artwork, music posters, and hundreds of old album covers, stapled to the ceiling and representing the eclectic mix of music you can hear at Shrine . . . and then some. Look up and see famous faces looking down on you. Nat Cole, Jerry Lee Lewis, Josephine Baker, Jerry Garcia, Marvin Gaye, Cyndi Lauper, Michael Jackson, Rod Stewart, Grace Slick. Quite a mix, no?

To your right is the cozy little bar of your idyllic music-club dreams, to your left a few café tables, and straight ahead a modest stage bathed in purple, blue, and green lights. The album covers crawl down the walls back there, a chandelier casts a subtle glow on them, and a jazz trio fills the room with soft sound.

Abdel and Sivan Ouedraogo (he from Burkina Faso in western Africa, she from Israel) opened Shrine in 2007 as a multimedia arts and culture venue where they could, Abdel says, "create something special uptown, and be a part of the art and live music scene."

"Walk in during the day to visit the venue and art exhibitions," he suggests. "We have different genres of live-music performances every night beginning at four p.m.—rock, jazz, African, Latin, reggae, blues, country, indie. From midnight to closing, we have different DJs playing all types of music for music lovers to dance to."

And that's the community Abdel and Sivan have fostered at Shrine: a family of music lovers from all over the city who go there like pilgrims, early and late, any day of the week, to be part of this special place. Often with no cover. Gotta love *that* in New York.

Shrine is a warm and lovely spot, and the staff and regulars will welcome you like part of their family. Abdel says that newcomers are struck by "the mix of customers from all races and backgrounds and the very friendly customer service. Our goal is to make you feel at home."

AS YOU MIGHT GUESS LOOKING AT THE SLIGHTLY REWORKED SIGN ABOVE ITS ENTRANCE, SHRINE TOOK OVER *the* SPOT ONCE OCCUPIED *by the* BLACK UNITED FUND, HARLEM'S LARGEST BLACK CHARITY GROUP. THE SIGN, ONE LETTER SHORT, NOW READS BLACK UNITED *FUN* PLAZA.

SHRINE

SO THIS WAS KIND *of a* BIG DEAL:
PRESIDENT OBAMA STOPPED *by* SHRINE *on* HIS SWING THROUGH HARLEM
A FEW WEEKS AFTER HIS FIRST INAUGURATION IN 2009.

WHEN TO GO	Sundays at five p.m., for the weekly jazz jam featuring Lu Reid. There's a less dense crowd than on Friday and Saturday nights, so you'll be able to kick it at the bar and check the place out, especially the eye-popping decor. After the jam, stick around and you might see anything: big band, reggae, punk, or even "hypnotic folk." Bonus: On Sundays there's no admission fee at the nearby Studio Museum of Harlem. It's one of the gems of the neighborhood, "internationally known for its catalytic role in promoting the works of artists of African descent." Check it out, then round out your cultural experience with live music at Shrine. *Happy hour: Monday to Saturday, 4 to 8 p.m. $3 draft beers, $5 frozen margaritas, $6 well drinks, and special prices on appetizers.*
WHERE TO SIT	Sit anywhere at the little bar, settle in, and enjoy a leisurely drink and a snack, from chips and guac or a cheese plate to grilled fish, grilled lamb chops, shish kebabs, or the Fela Burger (named after the Nigerian musician and activist Fela Kuti and topped with sautéed eggplant, red peppers, onions, and cheddar). "When you're done," says Abdel, "take two steps away from the bar and dance to the live music or DJs."
WHAT TO DRINK	Start off with a Henny Colada. Why? "It's the best Hennessy Colada in town!" as the lady next to us at the bar said. My wife couldn't ignore an endorsement like that and relished her piña colada made with Hennessy cognac in place of the standard rum. Next get something from Shrine's cocktail menu, such as the Baron, a bright, bubbly, brandy-based riff on a French 75 that takes Sivan's maiden name.

Henny Colada

2 ounces Hennessy cognac
2 ounces coconut cream
2 ounces pineapple juice

Combine all the ingredients in a blender with ice and blend until smooth. Pour into a sexy piña colada glass. Top with a maraschino cherry and a pineapple slice.

Shrine's Baron Cocktail

2 ounces Rémy Martin VSOP
    brandy
¾ ounce fresh lemon juice
¾ ounce simple syrup (equal parts
    water and sugar, stirred or
    shaken until the sugar completely
    dissolves)
Sparkling white wine

Shake the brandy, lemon juice, and simple syrup in a cocktail shaker with ice until well chilled. Strain into a cocktail glass and top with sparkling wine.

Subway: The 2, 3, B, and C trains stop at 135th Street, a one- or three-block walk to Shrine, respectively.

The old album covers all over the ceiling. You just don't get to see so many of these wonderful relics in one place very often. The Dazz Band, Janet Jackson, Men at Work, and *West Side Story*, the movie soundtrack. George Benson, Dave Brubeck, Charlie Barnet, and the *Beverly Hills Cop II* soundtrack. Abdel's favorites include Peter Tosh, Michael Jackson, Prince, and Fela Kuti's *Black President*. I was thrown back in time when I spotted Eddie Murphy from his eponymous 1982 standup comedy album grinning down on me.

STAN'S SPORTS BAR

836 River Avenue (at East 158th Street)   CONCOURSE VILLAGE, THE BRONX
stanssportsbar.com   ·   *718-993-5548*

IF YOU'RE GOING TO A BALL GAME, the point is to get riled up and have a good time, right? This is why we go to games—to be social, to yell, to eat junk food, to drink beer, and to get caught up in the noise and energy of a crowd. Otherwise, you may as well stay at home and do the crossword, occasionally glancing up at the TV for the score. *Lame.*

Look, if you're going to a game at Yankee Stadium, go big. Make a day of it. Go early, go to Stan's, belly up to the bar, order a beer, and get caught up in the excitement. Get into it, man. Feel the enthusiasm build. Are the Yankees winning? Good. Are they in a slump? Tough. You've got your expensive tickets, now enjoy the hell out of this day with your friends.

Stan's is only open on Yankee Stadium's event days, so with eighty-one regular-season home games, some soccer, a few concerts, and the occasional papal visit, that comes to about ninety to one hundred days a year, according to co-owner Mike Rendino. Typically, they open their doors about three hours before game time and stay open for one or two hours after the last out.

Before the game, it's pandemonium in Stan's, so you'd better have your big-boy pants on. It's loud. Even the music at full blast is regularly drowned out by the roar of the overhead trains rumbling by out front. The crowd's loud, too. Capacity is 270, but the oval bar is huge and takes up a lot of room, so the crowd feels even larger. *People!* People *everywhere!* You and 269 others: beefy, thick-necked Staten Island dudes, rich Manhattan girls in cutesy pink Yankees hats, tourists in their brand-new Yanks jerseys. *Tons* of Jeter merch everywhere you look. The Man himself filmed part of Gatorade's operatic "My Way" commercial at Stan's, and there's a signed picture behind the bar to prove it.

Visually, Stan's is like an indoor Times Square when the joint is jumping. There's neon signage everywhere: *Budweiser! Bud Light! Yankees! Heineken! Coors! Blue Moon! Budweiser! Brooklyn Lager! Miller Lite! Pabst!* And did I mention *Budweiser!* All the TVs are on, flags and banners hang above you, Stan's T-shirts hang everywhere *around* you, and light sconces that look like aluminum baseball bats dangle from the ceiling.

It's crazy, but good. This is why we go to ball games—for the spectacle. It's oddly comfortable at Stan's, once you get acclimated, not as cramped or stuffy or hot as you might think, especially toward the back, behind the bar and out of the fray. They removed several of the large windows in 2007, so on nice days when the gates are rolled up, that Bronxy-fresh breeze wafts in, and you get an indoor/outdoor, porch-like thing happening. It's summer in New York, and people are loving their day.

It's crazy, but good. This is why we go to ball games — for the spectacle.
It's oddly comfortable at Stan's, once you get acclimated, not as cramped or stuffy or hot
as you might think, especially toward the back, behind the bar and out of the fray.

STAN'S SPORTS BAR

Before the game, everyone's hunkered down in Stan's, together, like a team in the dugout, getting ready, anticipating the first pitch. Tension builds and builds and then, at game time, *boom*. Everyone bolts out of there and beelines to the stadium.

WHEN <u>TO</u> GO	Before any home game, especially, says Rendino, a game at four on Saturday afternoon. On those days, Stan's opens at ten in the morning and people come in early for a good, long pregame party before heading over to the stadium.
WHERE <u>TO</u> SIT	Don't sit, *stand*. Choose the far side of the bar, so you're facing the street and sidewalk across the bar, and toward the crowd streaming by.
WHAT <u>TO</u> DRINK	Start with a big, cold beer. How about a Coors in a tall, twenty-four-ounce can? That's pretty big, bro. Next drink: another beer. Why mess with success?
HOW <u>TO</u> GET THERE	Subway: Take the 4, B, or D to 161st Street–Yankee Stadium.
WHAT ELSE?	You can't help but notice the wall of caricatures in the back of the room, beyond the bar, featuring murals of the Babe, DiMaggio, Mickey, Yogi, Reggie, Jeter, and more. "Those were done by an artist from California, guy named Jason," Rendino says. "Don't know his last name. He worked here one summer a few years back, doing some bar-backing and bartending. Didn't know a thing about baseball! Had no idea who these guys were that he was painting." Still, he did a pretty good job. See if you can name them all. Stan's was opened back in 1998 by Stan Martucci, who owned the baseball memorabilia store next door. A teetotaler, Martucci was more into baseball merchandise than the bar business, but the bar next to his shop went up for sale, he bought it, and his timing was impeccable. The Yankees were near the beginning of a run of six trips to the World Series in eight seasons. Those were the days. . . .

How We Found Our Local

In 2006, my wife, Colleen, and I moved from the cozy Midwest college town of Ann Arbor to Manhattan, a big leap in geography, scale, and municipal temperament. We lived near Lincoln Center, a neighborhood more like bustling midtown to its south than the brownstoney Upper West Side to its north, and we never gained traction (or even recognition) at the local bars and restaurants. After three years, we moved to Brooklyn, its modest personality, lower population density, and toned-down energy level more to our liking.

We landed a fine apartment in Brooklyn Heights, a gorgeous old neighborhood directly across the East River from lower Manhattan, and, after some concerted looking, we found our local: Pete's Waterfront Ale House on Atlantic Avenue, a perfect blend of bar and restaurant. Pete's was a lively tavern with scruffy charm, like a lovable mutt, loaded after work with happy hour regulars and an early dinner rush of parents and kids. It was our own perfect little cocktail party on retainer, there any weeknight at six, just a couple of minutes' walk from our apartment. It didn't happen automatically. The key to becoming regulars at the Ale House was getting to know the staff.

David Qassim, one of our favorite waiters, was our gateway to regulardom. He liked us, we liked him, and he introduced us—sort of *vouched* for us—to the other servers and the bartenders. We were good customers, and the staff got to know us by name, eventually introducing us to other patrons. After a year or two, we became part of the Waterfront family. We met more regulars, made friends with several, got invited to their parties, and invited them to ours. We'd found the perfect local! Then the boss sold it. Closed nearly a year for renovations, it reopened as a slick pizza restaurant and lost a lot of its good old regulars' vibe and crowd.

But another place had recently opened half a block away.

The Long Island Bar (see page 124) on Atlantic Avenue and Henry Street had been closed since 2007, then reopened in 2013 as one of the best bars I've ever drunk a drink in, solid from top to bottom: cocktails, food, decor, service, and staff. We were charter members, showing up three times during the first week they opened. We got to know the staff and owners and received the honor of the second "most regular regulars," our credit card having apparently been used more than all but one during the LIB's first year back in business. It was a distinction we happily accepted, after a brief moment of shock, as in, *Did we really booze it up* that *much in here? Really?? Wow . . .*

No shame, though. Who could blame us? It's only a block from our place, this heavenly tavern, and the staff knows not only our names, but who we *are*. We never get greeted like Norm did on *Cheers* (which was, frankly, a bit coarse anyway, so, *fine*), but always with a smile, wave, handshake, or hug, and, from bartender Phil Ward, the inevitable wisecrack served up with a beardy grin. We'll take that and consider it an honor.

SUNNY'S BAR

253 Conover Street (between Beard and Reed Streets)   RED HOOK, BROOKLYN
sunnysredhook.com   ·   *718-625-8211*

FOR A WHILE IT WAS TOUCH AND GO, but now it's a good bet that Sunny's will still be around when you're reading this. I want everyone to experience Sunny's, though many of the place's regulars would throttle me for that. It's an out-of-the-way bar in an out-of-the-way neighborhood, and they like it that way.

It's a special place, Sunny's—a survivor. Been right there on Conover Street near the waterfront since Raffaele Balzano opened it in the late eighteen nineties. Seen plenty of ups and downs as the neighborhood changed, Red Hook's waterfront shipping boom giving way to decay in the seventies and eighties, then roaring back to life as the artists moved into the neighborhood, then the hipsters, the renovators, the families, and, of course, the real estate brokers, as Brooklyn and this formerly industrial neighborhood got hot.

That brings us to the bar's future. As I write this, Tone Johansen, Sunny Balzano's widow, just negotiated a triple bank shot and bought the eighteen fifties building—highly valued, as New York's real estate boom keeps a-booming—from seventeen of Sunny's surviving relatives. Not an easy task. "It's my calling to save this place," she says.

And Johansen has always come through in tough times. Like when she and Sunny (grandson of the bar's founder) worked for years negotiating government bureaucracy to make the speakeasy-like joint street legal, bringing the old building up to code and finally getting all the permits and licenses up-to-date. Then in 2012, Hurricane Sandy hit, knocking the old waterfront bar on its ass for about a year. But Tone and Sunny, with help from hundreds of friends, customers, and online contributors, got the place up and running again, stronger than ever.

After Sunny died in 2016, several members of his extended family hoped to sell the building at 253 Conover, as well as the one next door, which many of them had grown up in. Given New York's real estate market, you can understand why. Buildings near the waterfront—and their lots—could go to a condo developer for millions. But that didn't happen to Sunny's. Johansen prevailed, and plans to run Sunny's for years to come. She sees it as her mission. "It's like cooking soup, and Sunny's is the pot," she says. "Add the right bands, the right bartenders, the lighting, the crowd, and it all comes together." And come together it does.

During the week—especially in cooler months—the crowd tends to be more local, with self-employed creatives, professionals, and off-duty bartenders drifting in for quiet drinks and pleasant tunes, sometimes DJ'd on the spot by a bartender or a regular with their phone or laptop plugged into the sound system, or someone spinning vinyl. On weekends you'll find a younger, rowdier crowd,

THE COLLECTION *of* BIG-HEADED CELEBRITY STATUES HIGH ON A SHELF ABOVE THE BACK END *of the* BAR ARE MY FAVORITES. YOU'LL SEE PLASTER VERSIONS *of* HUMPHREY BOGART, MARK TWAIN, LOUIS ARMSTRONG, MAE WEST, AND . . . WHO'S THE LONG-HAIRED CHAP *with the* RED SHIRT *and* SUSPENDERS NEXT TO JIMMY DURANTE? IT'S . . . SUNNY BALZANO HIMSELF! THE SCULPTURE WAS SPECIALLY MADE AS A GIFT *by* A LONGTIME CUSTOMER *and* FRIEND.

beelining to Red Hook from all over New York for the live music at Sunny's. That's generally an open, good-natured scene, but it can be crowded, usually enjoyably so.

The place has heart. Yes, it's a historic waterfront dive, loaded with a good many weird and wonderful gewgaws, gimcracks, and whatnots, and I love that. But Sunny's also has immense *soul*, thanks in large part to its rich past and Sunny Balzano's warm, loving, mythically generous spirit. It's also due to the wildly popular live-music nights. Johansen, a Norwegian island girl from a musical Pentecostal family, worked for years to build up the bar's music scene, its heart, which pumps enormous vitality and joy from the little back room where many of the shows take place. This force permeates the whole bar, and you might even feel it resonating during quiet hours in the late afternoon.

"It's a collection of human energy," Johansen says. "You don't have that 'alone' feeling here, even when you're by yourself." She takes socializing as she does most things: seriously. "To be social," she says, "is a basic human need. There's a reason why solitary confinement is a punishment. Sunny's is all about people. It's about the human connection. It's a recharge station."

WHEN TO GO	If you want a quiet time to really *see* the place, show up late afternoon, when the light is good and you have room to roam. But to *really feel* the soul of Sunny's, you've got to catch some live music. Most nights, musicians and audiences crowd—sometimes at a nearly one-to-one ratio—into what Johansen calls the "proportionately perfect" back room or up in front, whipping up a frenzy of joy and sonic therapy that'll renew your spirit. You can't go wrong with the weekly bluegrass/folk and country jam every Saturday night at nine, and if you can catch the guitar wizards behind Smokey's Round Up or Stevie from St. Lou, or the luscious singing of Mara Kaye, you're in for a real treat. There's never a cover charge, but you'll want to tip the musicians. *Generously*. Good karma, and Sunny would be pleased.
WHERE TO SIT	Johansen says it's the seat in the farthest corner of the bar, next to the wall, "with your back to the kitchen. From there you can see the whole length of the bar." I agree that's a fine seat, but sometimes I'll take the fourth or fifth stool from the door as you walk in, and bask in the orange light of the setting sun.
WHAT TO DRINK	Go for a beer and a shot, an homage to the *berlermakers* (as Sunny called them, in the old Brooklyn style), the drink of *cherce* of the dockworkers who used to pack the place. Order the special and you'll usually get a cold can of Narragansett lager and a shot of Early Times whiskey. Not to be missed: hot buttered rum (when in season).

Sunny's Hot Buttered Rum

2 ounces dark rum
2 to 3 ounces hot buttered rum
*   batter (recipe follows)*
Hot water, just under a berl—er,
*   boil*

Combine the rum and batter in a sturdy mug, preferably an old reddish-brown one from a seventies-era diner with no fewer than one chip in its finish. Stir vigorously to combine and thin the batter. Top off with hot water and stir again.

Hot Buttered Rum Batter
Prepare in advance and use all winter.

1 pound butter
1 pound granulated sugar
1 pound brown sugar
1 tablespoon ground cinnamon
1 teaspoon ground cloves
1 teaspoon ground nutmeg
1 quart vanilla ice cream, softened
*   slightly*

Put all the ingredients except the ice cream in a large bowl and stir to combine. Add the ice cream and stir again. Transfer to a container with a lid, seal, and store in the freezer.

Author and former bartender Tim Sultan called Sunny's "a bar on the edge of the world" in the subtitle of his excellent 2016 book *Sunny's Nights,* and that pretty much sums up what it's like getting there. You can take the Wall Street Pier 11 South Brooklyn ferry to the Atlantic Basin in Red Hook, or with patience, the B61 bus, which runs along Van Brunt Street a block away. If I were you, though, I'd take a car. A steady stream of cars for hire and taxicabs on music nights says I'm not the only one who thinks so.

There's a lot to notice at Sunny's, especially when the late-afternoon light shoots all the way through the long front room, like solstice at Stonehenge, illuminating everything. You'll see a collection of Edwardian-era cheesecake pinup girls, a sort of banjo made from a bedpan, the helpful AVENUE P sign pointing the way to the commodes, and Johansen's favorite: a little statue of an old-time boxer in a tiny ring, "He represents the old Red Hook," she says, "where you had to fight your way through life."

TOOKER ALLEY

793 Washington Avenue (between St. John's and Lincoln Places) PROSPECT HEIGHTS, BROOKLYN
tookeralley.com · *347-955-4743*

"IF YOU WALK INTO A BAR AND THERE'S A CHEAP BEER OPTION, you know that everyone has a place at the table," says Tooker Alley's owner, Del Pedro. "It's just a bar," he says. "Not a snooty cocktail emporium." A man of his word, Pedro makes certain his place always offers a good old cheap beer option, lately a tallboy of Ballantine ale, an old-school brew you don't see much these days.

Pedro carries a torch for the Common Man, the proletariat, the working stiff, and the artwork displayed in Tooker Alley reflects that. To the left, hanging on the exposed brick as you walk in, you'll see a large photo taken at an Industrial Workers of the World march around 1920. A young man looking straight into the camera wears a fedora displaying a BREAD OR REVOLUTION card in its band. In the back of the long, narrow barroom, there's a framed poster featuring a grinning skull in a World War I doughboy helmet, smoking a cigarette. It was made for an antiwar dance sponsored by the Dil Pickle Club (yes, one *L*), a loose group of lefties, workers, liberated women, writers, kooks, commies, intellectuals, swells, and bums who formed a pro-labor, pro-peace, fun-loving, bohemian salon in Chicago in the early twentieth century. All were welcome in their little clubhouse tucked away on Tooker Alley in Chicago's Near North side, and Pedro lifted the name.

The name and philosophy behind his Tooker Alley were, as Pedro says, "a reaction to Bloomberg New York. I wanted this to be a place of racial and economic diversity, where you meet people unlike you, like on the subway. There's all kinds of diversity around here! Diversity makes bars *dynamic*, places where you can meaningfully encounter other people."

And encounter them you will at Tooker Alley. The people hanging out there run the gamut of age and race. It's a good-natured, comfortable, unfussy place, with some of the friendliest young bartenders I've ever met in Brooklyn, all sporting vests and ties, not to be fancy-pants, but out of respect for their craft and clientele.

You'll always hear good jazz playing at Tooker Alley, too. Pedro insists on it. Mostly hard bop from artists like John Coltrane, Horace Silver, and Miles Davis, then, when the place is "really buzzing," bebop from Bird, Monk, Diz, and the gang.

"It might not be your *everyday* place, but we can be *one* of your neighborhood bars," Pedro says. And he means it. He wants everyone in Prospect Heights and the surrounding area to feel welcome. "You can use it as you see fit," he says. "The place is at your disposal."

"Diversity makes bars dynamic, places where you can meaningfully encounter other people."

It's a good-natured, comfortable, unfussy place, WITH *some of the friendliest young bartenders I've ever met* IN *Brooklyn, all sporting vests and ties not to be fancy-pants, but out of respect* FOR *their craft* AND *clientele.*

WHEN TO GO

Pop in on a weeknight, right after the bar opens at five, when, Pedro says, "It's really mellow and sweet, and you feel like you've left the city behind. It's a serene time to have a cocktail."

WHERE TO SIT

The rightmost seat at the bar against the wall. There, you have the perfect spot to watch the bartenders do their thing, and an unimpeded view of the whole place.

WHAT TO DRINK

Start with a Tooker Alley stalwart, the Woody Guthrie, a rum cocktail developed by Pedro himself. Follow that up with an Amethyst, a suave little concoction made with tequila, genever, Marie Brizard parfait amour liqueur, and vermouth. On a budget? Get a can of that "cheap beer," or the beer-and-shot special.

HOUSE RECIPES

Woody Guthrie Cocktail

1 slice McIntosh apple
¾ ounce fresh lemon juice
¾ ounce simple syrup (equal parts sugar and water, stirred or shaken until the sugar completely dissolves)
1¾ ounces El Dorado 12-year-old rum
¾ ounce ginger beer
¼ ounce Clear Creek pear brandy
1 dash of Angostura bitters
1 ounce J.K. Scrumpy hard cider

In a cocktail shaker, muddle the apple slice with the lemon juice and simple syrup. Pour in the rum, ginger beer, brandy, and bitters and dry shake (without ice), then strain into a 10-ounce highball glass filled with ice. Add the cider and stir lightly. Garnish with the muddled apple slice and some candied ginger skewered on two toothpicks.

TOOKER ALLEY

Amethyst Cocktail

1¾ ounces Sauza Hornitos blanco
    tequila
½ ounce Marie Brizard parfait
    amour liqueur
½ ounce Bols Genever gin
1 teaspoon Martini & Rossi bianco
    vermouth
¼ teaspoon simple syrup (equal
    parts water and sugar, stirred or
    shaken until the sugar completely
    dissolves)

Add the ingredients to a mixing glass full of cracked ice. Stir until well chilled and strain into a "Nick and Nora" cocktail glass. Sip suavely while exchanging droll bon mots with cinematic precision.

HOW TO GET THERE

Subway: The 2 and 3 trains stop at the Eastern Parkway–Brooklyn Museum station, a three-minute walk away.

WHAT ELSE?

A little about the Dil Pickle Club, whose philosophy inspired Del Pedro's vision for Tooker Alley (from the bar's website):

In the city of Chicago, from 1915 till about 1930, a complete cross section of early industrial America squeezed itself "through the hole in the wall, down Tooker Alley" in search of "the Green Lite over the Orange Door." On that door was scrawled "Step High, Stoop Low, Leave Your Dignity Outside" and behind it lay a most peculiar institution—the Dil Pickle Club.

Consciously nobrow, militantly inclusive, and ceaselessly creative, the Dil Pickle Club eschewed any and all social, economic, or cultural limitations. . . .

Although never itself a bar, The Dil Pickle Club embodied all the elements that any self-respecting bar would want: a crowd drawn from all quarters of society; a high-spirited atmosphere; free-flowing banter; and, finally, pure and simple fun. As "founder and janitor" Jack Jones would say, "If you're a nut about anything then you have to meet the Picklers."

It is from this memorable place that Tooker Alley takes both its name and inspiration. Tooker Alley hopes to bring together consumption, culture, and community in an integrated way that we feel is given short shrift nowadays. It is a bar that, as the denizens of the Dil Pickle Club so brilliantly put it, "elevates your mind to a lower level of thinking."

Honorable Mentions

When my editor told me that Rizzoli wanted fifty—count 'em: *fifty*—bar profiles for this book, I paused. I'd proposed twenty-five originally, and they wanted double that.

It wasn't tough to hit that number. New York is home to thousands of bars, and believe me, plenty of them are worthy. The real trick was actually narrowing it down to a *mere* fifty.

Every neighborhood in every borough is home to bars, taverns, and dives that people love. Places that locals call their locals and well-known spots that folks come from all over the city to visit. I couldn't include them all, so here's a short list of some other places worth a visit.

4TH AVENUE PUB
(Boerum Hill, Brooklyn)

This narrow, friendly local pub sits on busy Fourth Avenue, just south of Brooklyn's Barclays Center. It's a perfect place to hang out after work, before a concert or game, or after a show at nearby BAM. Good craft beer selection, friendly service, free popcorn and a well-appointed backyard beer garden. Happy hour to boot: $1 off everything, Monday to Friday, 3 to 8 p.m. *76 Fourth Avenue*

ABILENE
(Carroll Gardens, Brooklyn)

Low-key local bar with huge open windows and sidewalk seating during most of the year. The kitchen puts out filling, affordable chow (burgers, salads, sandwiches, nachos, and some pretty durn good onion rings, too) all day long with a popular brunch on weekends. Bonus points: Ice-cold Miller High Life bottles for $3 are there when you need 'em. *442 Court Street*

ATTABOY
(Lower East Side, Manhattan)

The coolest, friendliest quality cocktail "speakeasy" you could ever hope for. This remarkable hidden gem serves up some of the absolute best cocktails in the city, all made with gracious hospitality by boss Sam Ross and a staff of beautiful ladies and gentlemen who have your comfort and needs first and foremost in mind. *134 Eldridge Street*

THE BAR ᴀᴛ JUNIOR'S RESTAURANT
(Downtown Brooklyn)

The place is known for its cheesecake and that's just fine, but after a show at nearby BAM (or any evening), I highly recommend a visit to the surprisingly hopping bar scene in the back part of the restaurant. You can order off the menu if you're hungry, and get anything you want to drink, made with good cheer by longtime bartender Rick McGillicuddy. Enjoy the rowdy crowd of regulars, too. *386 Flatbush Avenue Ext.*

BAR BRUNO
(Carroll Gardens, Brooklyn)

A friendly corner cantina with a Mexican-leaning menu and a soccer bar–ish vibe. (They're big fans of the great George Best here, as you'll see from the outdoor mural, pictures on the walls, cheeky Best quotes, etc.) The small bar is a perfect place to enjoy taco Tuesday with one of their many michelada options, and when weather permits, the sidewalk cafe on this leafy residential corner is picture-perfect. *520 Henry Street*

CODY'S
(Cobble Hill, Brooklyn)

Just a clean, comfortable neighborhood sports bar, loaded with TVs, with a full complement of cable channels. Just ask, and they'll likely put on any game you want to see, and cheerfully so. Grab a seat, order up some suds, fried goodies, and nachos, and get your game on, big guy. *154 Court Street*

FOREST HILLS STATION
(Forest Hills, Queens)

A lively neighborhood tavern right by the LIRR station in this leafy part of Queens. You'll find a beautiful after-work/dinner scene here, and some of the best bar food I've had the pleasure of devouring during the research for this book. *106-11 Seventy-first Avenue*

JUST LORRAINE'S PLACE
(Harlem, Manhattan)

A friendly, no-frills neighborhood sports bar. The mostly older, mostly black regulars welcome you at a modest bar, where you receive stiff pours and—if you're lucky—paper plates full of salty munchies, gratis. *2247 Adam Clayton Powell Jr. Boulevard*

THE LOEB BOATHOUSE CAFÉ
(Central Park, Manhattan)

A great good place in the original way Henry James meant it in his 1900 short story, as a respite from the noise and clatter of the modern world. The Boathouse sits on the lake in Central Park, surrounded by trees, birds, and fresh (for New York) air. The outdoor café is a lovely place to rejuvenate on a warm day, especially during the week or off-hours, when the crowds are thinner and you can get a seat by the water. *East Seventy-second Street*

LUCEY'S LOUNGE
(South Slope, Brooklyn)

A wonderfully eccentric little bar near the gritty intersection of Brooklyn's old industrial Gowanus neighborhood and South Slope. Inventive drinks and smart design (sliding hooks for purses and bags under the bar, for instance, and a footrest at the bar that heats up in the winter) set this cozy enclave apart from the others. *475 Third Avenue*

MIKE'S PUB
(Woodhaven, Queens)

A big, divey throwback of a workingman's Irish pub in the great Queens tradition. With its zero frills, low prices, and unabashedly lowbrow clientele, Archie Bunker would have loved this place, and thanks to the friendly, welcoming bartenders, so do I. *79-19 Jamaica Avenue*

QUARTER BAR
(South Slope, Brooklyn)

A comfy local bar that serves up an unpretentious-but-perfect cocktail as easily as a pint of good beer. Bonus points for a flowery backyard and boss David Moo's topnotch hostmanship, which helped Quarter earn a "Best Bar in America" nod from *Esquire* magazine in 2016. *676 Fifth Avenue*

THE RICHARDSON
(Williamsburg, Brooklyn)

This slick, friendly corner bar sits just the other side of the Brooklyn Queens Expressway. Though technically in Williamsburg, it's more local than the Bedford/Berry/Wythe Street crowds, and an excellent brunch or afternoon option when you want to get away from the crush of shopping-bag-toting European tourists that has turned so much of Williamsburg into a weekend scene like Manhattan's Soho shopping extravaganza. *451 Graham Avenue*

THE ROOFTOP of FORNINO
(Brooklyn Bridge Park, Brooklyn Heights)

You can almost always get a seat here on any beautiful day that they're open (it's seasonal, so check first), enjoy a reasonably priced beer or cocktail, kick back, and watch the sunset over New York harbor as day slips into night and you munch on fresh pizza just out of their wood-fired oven. *Pier 6, Brooklyn Bridge Park*

THE SHANTY
(Williamsburg, Brooklyn)

This industrial-chic, full-service bar sits right off the distilling room at New York Distilling Company's operation in Williamsburg, Brooklyn. Stop at the Shanty and escape Williamsburg's frenetic tourist scene. Have a beautiful cocktail made with one of the house gins, and, if you're lucky, catch a little live music. *79 Richardson Street*

SPUYTEN DUYVIL
(Williamsburg, Brooklyn)

This place is beer-geek heaven. A snug, oddly shaped joint with maps on the walls and vintage curios everywhere. They've got a thoughtful little tap selection, a hell of a lot of bottles, happy hour, a diverse jukebox, and a gorgeous, quiet, leafy backyard. *359 Metropolitan Avenue*

ST. GAMBRINUS

(Downtown Brooklyn)

A damned delightful little beer-geek bar where you can sample sixteen fresh, unusual beers on tap, and enjoy a piping hot pressed sandwich (absolutely delicious) as well. Oh, and they have a large backyard where you can tipple in the shade of large, leafy trees. AND they sell bottles, cans, and growlers to go. OH, AND the service offers that easy, smart charm of people who know what they're selling, and like to talk about it. (Obviously I love this place.) *533 Atlantic Avenue, Brooklyn*

STATION CAFÉ

(Woodside, Queens)

This old-school Irish shot–and–beer joint, tucked under the Woodside–61st Street train station, is a great spot for happy hour on the way home. Cheap drinks, friendly bartenders, and a pool table round out a perfectly Queensy dive bar experience. *39-50 Sixty-first Street*

THREE'S BREWING

(Gowanus, Brooklyn)

This fine brewing operation features not only several of their own beers, but other local and regional taps as well, along with a full-service coffee bar run by Ninth Street Espresso, a kitchen with rotating pop-up purveyors, and a sweet backyard. *333 Douglass Street*

TILE BAR

(East Village, Manhattan)

An unpretentious, inexpensive, more-or-less civilized throwback to the older days of the East Village, when it was defined more by intellect and creativity than wealth and fashion. Tile Bar is still a local hangout, despite its central EV location, and after work the locals still come in, grab a cheap beer, and argue about politics, books, and movies. *115 First Avenue*

TØRST

(Greenpoint, Brooklyn)

A sleek, high-tech beer bar that feels like a lounge at a Scandinavian airport, and I mean that in a good way. There is nothing extraneous about this place. The service is impeccable, the music is on point, and the boutique selection of beers is nurtured to perfection by their "flux capacitor" system, which maintains freshness through automatic regulation of each keg's temperature and CO_2 pressure. *615 Manhattan Avenue*

THE WHARF

(Rockaway Park, Queens)

Tucked behind a Shell station is this surprise: a waterfront bar on Jamaica Bay. Boats pull up to the docks, ruddy-faced locals pound macrobeers at the outdoor bar, and a Buffet/Marley soundtrack ushers in spectacular sunsets. *416 Beach 116th Street*

INDEX BY BOROUGH

THIS BOOK CAME TO BE IN A LUCKY ROUNDABOUT WAY.

It all goes back to an art project I started in 2013, drawing and making silkscreen prints of a handful of my favorite bars in Brooklyn. I was inspired to do this by my artsy colleague Molly Morlock and urban artists such as Eric Rewitzer, Paul Madonna, James Michalopoulos, and the late, great Milton Kemnitz.

I completed a series of these pieces and showed them in Brooklyn at Fort Defiance in Red Hook (thanks to the boss, St. John Frizell) and the Long Island Bar in Cobble Hill (hats off to owners Toby Cecchini and Joel Tompkins).

After these shows, the idea to do a book was bandied about by both Eric Schmid and Tony Biancosino. Skeptical, I checked in with Susanna Einstein, the agent of my friend, author Lara Zielin. Susanna introduced me to her then partner Meg Thompson, who handled nonfiction. I schlepped a portfolio of prints and a few of the wall labels from my shows down to their office, Meg signed me as a client, then landed me a book deal with the fabulous Rizzoli Publications of New York. Simple.

Inspiration for the direction of the book came from great authors like Joe Mitchell and Pete Hamill, who wrote so well about the places they loved. Then there's Jane and Michael Stern and Pableaux Johnson, who brought their favorite restaurants and bars to life with punchy writing and delicious phrasing. And, of course, Ray Oldenburg, who wrote about why "third places" like neighborhood bars matter so much to begin with, in his classic *The Great Good Place*.

Then the research began. I had to find another forty-some bars worthy of drawing and writing about—places I could honestly say New Yorkers loved, that I approved of, too. This meant gathering leads, getting out to neighborhoods in all five boroughs, and visiting—sometimes multiple times—north of 150 places, and for this I've got to thank my bar sherpas, guides, and helper-livers.

Thank you Jeff Sword and Jon Washburn, who showed me some of the best spots in Brooklyn way back before I even lived here. Roger Hitts and Al Rodriguez, who hopped all over Queens with my wife, Colleen, and me. Staten Island: Are you kidding? I wouldn't have known where to start without Juan Villafana and Tony Marceda, who covered it with us from tip to tail, designated-driving for us. Dave Pappas gave us a comprehensive tour of his neighborhood, Bay Ridge. Twyla Sevcik and Brian Ralston made a day of exploring Coney Island with us. We trekked up to the Bronx with Bridget Rohde and Brian Mich a couple of times. Then there's a rotating cast of friends and drinking buddies who helped me hit one-offs here and there during this project: Mike Sorgatz, Merrick Modeste, Jimmy Luma, Al and Joyce Jaffee, Jordan Hirsch, Lisa Gauchey, Rick Midler, Chuck Loesner, Mark Roth, and . . . oh, geez. A bunch of others, I'm sure of it. Details are fuzzy. Ask again later.

Thanks to Rob Hess, who suggested I write this book like I was personally telling him about cool places to visit. When I was stuck, his advice helped me find my voice. And thanks to Charles Cole, who graciously allowed me to use his studio, enabling me to get the job done.

Thank you to Caitlin Leffel, who acquired my book at Rizzoli and helped give it its initial shape; to Sarah Scheffel, who did a great job fine-tuning my words; to Tricia Levi, who helped shepherd the project over the finish line; and to designer Sebit Min, who made it look amazing. Also a hat-tip to James Carpenter, for his excellent proofreading.

And of course, predictably, the biggest thanks goes to Colleen, who gets more beautiful (and tolerant) every year, and who sacrificed many a decent night's sleep, jeans that fit, and countless brain cells with her cheerful, insightful, and dedicated research assistance from the start of the project to the very end, when she served as my primo copyeditor. Love ya, darlin'.

Thank you one and all. [*Clink!*]. You rule!